T0115974

THE
EXPLOSIVE
CHILD

ALSO BY ROSS GREENE, PH.D.

Lost at School
Lost & Found
Raising Human Beings

THE
EXPLOSIVE
CHILD

SIXTH EDITION

**A New Approach for Understanding and
Parenting Easily Frustrated, Chronically
Inflexible Children**

Ross W. Greene, Ph.D.

HARPER

NEW YORK • LONDON • TORONTO • SYDNEY

HARPER

This book is written as a source of information only and should not be considered a substitute for the advice, decisions, or judgment of a qualified mental health professional. All efforts have been made to ensure the accuracy of the information contained in this book as of the date published. The author and the publisher expressly disclaim responsibility for any adverse effects arising from the use or application of the information contained herein.

THE EXPLOSIVE CHILD. Copyright © 1998, 2000, 2005, 2010, 2014, 2021 by Ross W. Greene, Ph.D. All rights reserved. Printed in the United States of America. No part of this book may be used or reproduced in any manner whatsoever without written permission except in the case of brief quotations embodied in critical articles and reviews. For information, address HarperCollins Publishers, 195 Broadway, New York, NY 10007.

HarperCollins books may be purchased for educational, business, or sales promotional use. For information, please email the Special Markets Department at SPsales@harpercollins.com.

All illustrations by Greg Daly

Library of Congress Cataloging-in-Publication Data has been applied for.

ISBN 978-0-06-309246-4 (pbk.)

24 25 26 27 28 LBC 21 20 19 18 17

In memory of my father, Irving A. Greene

Anyone can become angry, that is easy . . .
but to be angry with the right person, to the right degree,
at the right time, for the right purpose, and in the right way . . .
this is not easy.

—ARISTOTLE

Do the best you can until you know better.
Then when you know better, do better.

—MAYA ANGELOU

CONTENTS

PREFACE

Welcome to the 2021 edition of *The Explosive Child*, which comes twenty-three years after the first edition was published in 1998. A lot has happened during those years. The book is now published in dozens of languages. The model described in these pages has undergone one decidedly uncollaborative name change. (It was originally named *Collaborative Problem Solving*, but is now called *Collaborative & Proactive Solutions*.) The CPS model has been implemented by hundreds of thousands of families and thousands of schools, in-patient psychiatry units, and residential and juvenile detention facilities throughout the world. Numerous published studies have documented its effectiveness, and it has been validated as an evidence-based intervention. Because of various refinements over the years, the model is easier to understand and implement. This edition reflects the most current iteration. In an effort to be sensitive to different preferences, the book is written using male, female, and gender nonspecific pronouns in alternating chapters.

I'll start off by acknowledging that I've never been a huge fan of the title of the book. *Explosive* is just a descriptive term for kids who become frustrated far more easily and more often than "ordinary" kids, and communicate their frustration in ways that are far more extreme (screaming, swearing, spitting, hitting, kicking, biting, cutting, destroying property). But *explosive* is a clumsy adjective for several reasons. First, it implies that the outbursts of these kids are sudden and unpredictable and—this may be a little hard to believe at first—that's actually not true most of the time. Second, while many kids explode when they're frustrated, many others *implode* instead (crying, sulking, whining, pouting, avoiding, withdrawing, or being worried or anxious). The title of the book notwithstanding, the strategies described herein are applicable to kids who are exploding, imploding, or some combination of the two.

But the behaviors aren't even the most important part. Rather, what those behaviors are *telling* us is the most important part. And what they're telling us is that your child is having *difficulty meeting certain expectations*. Some kids withdraw when there are expectations they're having difficulty meeting (otherwise they don't withdraw). Other kids hit when there are expectations they're having difficulty meeting (otherwise they don't hit). While it's tempting to focus on your child's *behaviors,* in this book we'll be focusing instead on the *expectations* they are having difficulty meeting that are causing those behaviors. That crucial distinction is going to make a world of difference.

One of the things you'll learn in the early chapters of the book is that the terms that have commonly been used to characterize kids with concerning behaviors—terms such as *willful, manipulative, attention-seeking, limit-testing, contrary, intransigent, unmotivated*—are inaccurate and counterproductive. You'll also read that a lot of the things we've been saying about the parents of these kids—that they're passive, permissive, inconsistent, noncontingent, inept disciplinarians—aren't accurate or productive either. And you'll learn that the psychiatric diagnoses that may have been applied to your child don't provide the information you need to accurately understand their difficulties and effectively help them.

This may sound a little strange, but there's never been a better time to be living or working with a child with concerning behaviors. That's because an enormous amount of research on kids with concerning behaviors has accumulated over the past fifty years, so we know a lot more about why and when they're struggling and how to help them than at any other point in human evolution. The research provides us with new lenses through which to view their difficulties, and those new lenses can help you respond to and help these kids in ways that are more compassionate, productive, and effective. That's the good news. The bad news is that the new lenses can take some getting used to (after all, there's a decent chance you've been wearing different lenses for a very long time). So, you'll need an open mind. Also, the strategies contained in this book can be quite a departure from the norm and may differ from the way you were raised, so they'll likely require some practice (and patience), as you and your child become accustomed to new ways of interacting and solving problems.

If you are the parent of a child with social, emotional, and behavioral challenges, this book should help you feel more optimistic about and confident in handling their difficulties, get you out of the business of "walking on eggshells" or being in "perpetual survival mode," and restore some sanity to your family. If you are the child's grandparent, teacher, neighbor, coach, or therapist, this book should, at the least, help you understand and, better yet, help you participate in the process of making things better.

There is no panacea. You have some hard work ahead of you. But you're working hard already. Let's make sure you have something to show for all that hard work.

ROSS W. GREENE, PH.D.
FREEPORT, MAINE

ACKNOWLEDGMENTS

This being the sixth rendition of this book, this is the sixth acknowledgment section I've written for it. And I'm still thankful to many of the same people. My kids Talia and Jacob—now twenty-three and twenty years old—continue to keep me on my toes and help me practice what I preach. My mom, still living it up in her golden years, is also still a source of wisdom and empathy. And the book is still dedicated to my father, who died long before the first edition was published.

This book wouldn't have been published without the vision and devotion of my friend and agent, Wendy Lipkind, who died in 2011. While I find myself wishing I could talk with her sometimes, I can still hear her sage wisdom whenever I think to ask for it.

My thinking about how to help kids and their adult caregivers get along better has been influenced by many parents, teachers, and supervisors. It was my incredible good fortune to be mentored by Dr. Thomas Ollendick while I was a graduate student in the clinical psychology program at Virginia Tech. Tom has remained a good friend and colleague for the past thirty years. Two mental health professionals who supervised me during my training years were particularly influential: Dr. George Clum (now retired from Virginia Tech) and Dr. Mary Ann McCabe (then at Children's National Medical Center in Washington, D.C.). Lorraine Lougee, a social worker at CNMC, gets credit for pushing me to take a strong stand on behalf of kids who need help. And I probably wouldn't have gone into psychology in the first place if I hadn't stumbled across the path of Dr. Elizabeth Altmaier when I was an undergraduate at the University of Florida (she moved on to the University of Iowa and is now retired).

However, those who were most central to the evolution of many of the ideas in this book, and to whom I owe the greatest debt of gratitude, were the many kids, parents, educators, and staff with whom I've had the privilege of working over the years. There are truly amazing people in this world who care deeply about improving the lives of kids, have embraced the Collaborative & Proactive Solutions (CPS) model, and, with vision, energy, and relentless determination, have advocated for greater compassion and empathy for kids with concerning behaviors and implementation of the

CPS approach in families, schools, clinics, inpatient units, and residential and juvenile detention facilities. It has been an honor to cross paths and work with you.

And, last but definitely not least, there's Jenny, who I adore.

1

THE WAFFLE EPISODE

Saturday morning. Jennifer, age eleven, wakes up, makes her bed, looks around her room to make sure everything is in its place, and heads into the kitchen to make herself breakfast. She peers into the freezer, removes the container of frozen waffles, and counts six waffles. Thinking to herself, "I'll have three waffles this morning and three tomorrow morning," Jennifer toasts her three waffles and sits down to eat.

Moments later, her mother, Debbie, and seven-year-old brother, Riley, enter the kitchen, and Debbie asks Riley what he'd like to eat for breakfast. Riley responds, "Waffles," and Debbie reaches into the freezer for the waffles. Jennifer, who has been listening and watching intently, explodes.

"He can't have the waffles!" Jennifer screams, her face suddenly reddening.

"Why not?" asks Debbie, her voice rising.

"I was going to have those waffles tomorrow morning!" Jennifer screams, jumping out of her chair.

"I'm not telling your brother he can't have waffles!" Debbie yells back.

"He can't have them!" screams Jennifer, now face to face with her mother.

Debbie, wary of the physical and verbal aggression of which her daughter is capable during these moments, desperately asks Riley if there might be something else he would consider eating.

"I want waffles," whimpers Riley, cowering behind his mother.

Jennifer, her frustration and agitation at a peak, pushes Debbie out of the way, seizes the container of frozen waffles, then slams the freezer door shut, grabs her plate of toasted waffles, and stalks to her room. Debbie and Riley begin to cry.

Jennifer's family members have endured hundreds of such episodes. In many instances, the episodes are more prolonged and intense and involve more physical or verbal aggression than the one just described (when Jennifer was eight, she kicked out a window of the family car). Doctors have bestowed myriad diagnoses on Jennifer, including oppositional-defiant disorder, bipolar disorder, intermittent explosive disorder, and disruptive mood dysregulation disorder. For Jennifer's parents, however, a simple label doesn't begin to capture the upheaval, turmoil, and trauma that her outbursts cause, and doesn't help them understand *why*

Jennifer acts the way she does or *when* the outbursts are likely to occur.

Debbie and Riley are scared of her. Jennifer's extreme volatility and inflexibility require constant vigilance and enormous energy from her mother and father, consuming attention the parents wish they could devote to Riley. Debbie and her husband, Kevin, frequently argue over the best way to handle her behavior but are in agreement about the strain Jennifer places on their marriage. Jennifer has no close friends; children who initially befriend her eventually find her rigid, bossy personality difficult to tolerate.

Over the years, Debbie and Kevin have sought help from countless mental health professionals, most of whom have urged them to set firmer limits and be more consistent in managing Jennifer's behavior, and have instructed them on how to implement formal reward and punishment strategies, usually in the form of sticker charts and time-outs. When such strategies failed to work, Jennifer was medicated with multiple combinations of drugs, without dramatic effect. After eight years of setting firmer limits, dutifully doling out happy faces, and administering a cornucopia of medicines, Jennifer has changed little since infancy, when there were clear signs that there was something "different" about her. In fact, her outbursts are more intense and more frequent than ever.

· · ·

"It is very humiliating to be scared of your own daughter," says Debbie. "People who don't have a child like Jennifer don't have a clue about what it's like to live like this. Believe me, this is not what I envisioned when I dreamed of having children. This is a nightmare.

"You can't imagine the embarrassment of having Jennifer 'lose it' around people who don't know her. I feel like telling them, 'I have another kid at home who doesn't act like this—I really am a good parent!'

"I know people are thinking, 'What wimpy parents she must have . . . what that kid really needs is a good thrashing.' Believe me, we've tried everything with her. But nobody's been able to tell us how to help her. No one's really been able to tell us what's the matter with her!

"I used to think of myself as a kind, patient, sympathetic person. But Jennifer has caused me to act in ways in which I never thought myself capable. I'm emotionally spent. I can't keep living like this. We are in a constant state of crisis.

"Each time I start to get my hopes up, each time I have a pleasant interaction with Jennifer, I let myself become a little optimistic and start to like her again . . . and then it all comes crashing down with her next outburst.

"I know a lot of other parents whose kids give them a little trouble sometimes. But Jennifer is in a completely different league! It makes me feel very alone."

Debbie and Kevin are definitely not alone; there are a lot of Jennifers out there. Their parents often discover that strategies that are commonly used with less difficult kids—such as explaining, reasoning, redirecting, insisting, reassuring, nurturing, ignoring, rewarding, and punishing—don't accomplish much with their Jennifers (and, for reasons that will soon make a great deal of sense, can actually make things worse). If you started reading this book because you have a Jennifer of your own, you're probably familiar with how frustrated, confused, angry, bitter, guilty, overwhelmed, spent, scared, and hopeless Jennifer's parents feel.

But there is hope, as long as the children's caregivers are willing to take a close look at their beliefs about the factors contributing to concerning behaviors and then apply strategies that are a far cry from discipline-as-usual. In other words, dealing more effectively with these kids requires, first and foremost, an *understanding* of why they're responding so poorly to problems and frustrations. In some instances, the understanding part can, by itself, lead to improvements in your interactions with your child, even before any formal strategies are tried.

Your new understanding of your child begins in the next chapter. The new strategies come after that.

• • •

Post-meltdown, Debbie sat glumly at the kitchen table, a lukewarm cup of coffee in front of her. Riley was at a friend's house. Jennifer was in her bedroom watching a movie, quiet for now. While Debbie wasn't ecstatic about the amount of time Jennifer spent in front of a screen, she felt it was a small price to pay for peace.

Her dilemma: whether to tell Kevin about the waffle episode. Kevin, a high school teacher, had been at the hardware store during the episode. Under normal circumstances, he was a calm, patient man. But he became a completely different person—screaming, threatening—when Jennifer turned life upside down in the family. He'd never totally lost control, but Debbie was concerned about what he'd do if that ever happened. (Kevin had left marks on Jennifer's arms back in the days when they'd tried restraining her and holding her in time-out. Debbie had since convinced him that physically restraining Jennifer was a bad idea.)

"I'm not letting that kid rule our lives," Kevin often fumed. *Famous last words*, Debbie thought to herself. If she told Kevin of the waffle episode, she risked having him storm down to Jennifer's room and impose a punishment—taking away her laptop seemed to be his default these days—which would simply ignite another blowout. But if she didn't tell him, Riley probably would, and then Kevin would accuse her of undermining him as an authority figure.

It was during these quiet times that Debbie tended to reflect on Jennifer, who was difficult the instant she came into the world. The nurses at the hospital forewarned that she and Kevin were in for quite a ride, and Debbie could still picture their smiling faces when they said it. "Freaking hysterical," she now muttered. There were the countless hours spent trying (often to no avail) to get Jennifer to stop crying as a baby. The three preschools that had decided Jennifer was beyond what they could handle. The early calls from the pre-K teachers about other kids not wanting to play with Jennifer because she was bossy and inflexible and tended to handle disagreements with physical aggression. There was the suggestion from the kindergarten teachers that Jennifer might benefit from testing or from therapy. There were the play therapists with their toys and dolls, the behavioral therapists with their time-outs and sticker charts, the psychiatrists with their medications, the play dates that went badly, the friendship groups Jennifer refused to attend, the diagnoses, the testing.

But most of all, there were still the outbursts.

Their minister urged Debbie to find time for herself. Kevin chuckled when he heard that suggestion: "All you do with your free time is think about Jennifer. You're obsessed." And he was right.

Debbie heard the front door open. "Hello," Kevin called from the front hallway. The hardware store always put him in a good mood.

"In here," called Debbie.

"Any coffee left?" asked Kevin as he came into the kitchen.

"A little," Debbie said, trying to sound far more chipper than she felt.

Kevin caught the tone in Debbie's voice. "What's the matter?" he said.

"Nothing," said Debbie.

"What'd she do?" Kevin demanded.

Here we go, thought Debbie. "Oh, we just had a little incident over waffles while you were gone."

"Waffles?"

"She and Riley both wanted the same waffles . . . not a big deal."

"Now she's blowing up over waffles? Geez, what's it gonna be next? Where is she?" Kevin's blood was beginning to boil.

"Kevin, I handled it. It's not a big deal. Really. You don't need to do anything."

"Did she hit you?"

"No, she did not hit me. Kevin, it's done."

"You swear she didn't hit you?" Kevin had become aware of his wife's tendency to downplay the severity of the outbursts that occurred when he wasn't around.

"She didn't hit me."

Kevin sighed loudly as he sat down dejectedly at the kitchen table. Debbie poured him what was left of the coffee.

"Where's Riley?"

"At Stevie's house."

"Did Jennifer hit him?"

"No. Kevin, there was no hitting. Just some screaming. It's really over."

"What's she doing in her room?"

"Watching a video."

"So, as usual, she blows up, and we reward her with a video."

"I've never noticed that depriving her of videos keeps her from blowing up the next time. I just wanted some peace."

"Peace," scoffed Kevin.

Debbie felt tears welling up in her eyes but pinched them away. "Let's just try to have a nice day."

"In this family, there is no such thing."

2

YOUR NEW LENSES HAVE ARRIVED

You know the things that are commonly said about kids who exhibit concerning behaviors: they're manipulative, attention-seeking, unmotivated, stubborn, willful, intransigent, bratty, spoiled, controlling, resistant, out of control, and defiant. There's more: they are skilled at testing limits, pushing buttons, coercing adults into giving in, and getting their way. You know (perhaps from personal experience) the things that are said about their parents: they're passive, permissive, inconsistent, neglectful, inept disciplinarians. They botched the job.

Don't believe any of it. First, most parents of kids with concerning behaviors have other children who are well-behaved, so unless they made the conscious decision to parent competently with one child and incompetently with another, blaming parents for a child's concerning behavior is a nonstarter. Second, kids who exhibit concerning behaviors don't exhibit those behaviors *all* the time, just *sometimes*. That's a very big deal, because it permits us to take a closer look at the specific *conditions* in which they're exhibiting concerning behaviors.

And what are those conditions? Quite simply, **when there are expectations they're having difficulty meeting**. If your child is having difficulty brushing his teeth before going to bed at night, that's a time when he's more likely to exhibit concerning behaviors. If he's having no difficulty meeting that expectation, it won't cause concerning behaviors. If your child is having difficulty getting started on or completing a particular homework assignment, that's a time when he's more likely to exhibit concerning behaviors. If he's having no difficulty meeting that expectation, it won't cause concerning behaviors.

Why does your child exhibit concerning behaviors more often and, perhaps, in ways that are more extreme than many other kids? The answer to that question comes from the research that has accumulated over the past fifty years on kids with concerning behaviors: **he's lacking crucial skills**.

Wait, he's lacking what?

He's lacking crucial skills. Kids who exhibit concerning behaviors are compromised in the global skills of *flexibility, adaptability, frustration tolerance, emotion regulation,* and *problem solving.* These are skills most of us take for granted. And most kids are blessed with sufficient levels of those skills. Your child was not so fortunate.

He's not lacking motivation? No, he's not. But a lot of folks still think that. Why haven't your efforts to motivate your child to behave more adaptively—with rewards and punishments—been successful? Because he isn't unmotivated. If your kid *could* respond to problems and frustrations adaptively, he *would.* That's because—and this is, without question, the most important theme of this entire book—***kids do well if they can***.

So, he's not exhibiting concerning behaviors on purpose? No. The kids about whom this book is written do not *choose* to exhibit concerning behaviors any more than a child would choose to have a reading disability. And, in fact, that is an apt comparison. Kids who are having difficulty reading are lacking the skills required for being proficient in reading. Kids who are having difficulty adaptively handling problems and frustrations are lacking the skills required for being proficient in handling problems and frustrations. A long time ago kids who had difficulty reading were referred to as lazy or stupid. Thankfully, that isn't the case anymore. But, way too often, we're still referring to kids with concerning behaviors in ways that are tragically inaccurate.

And he's not exhibiting concerning behaviors because he just wants his own way? We all want our own way, so that's a nonstarter, too. Getting your own way adaptively requires some very important skills.

The *kids do well if they can* philosophy is important for another reason. See, a different mentality—*kids do well if they want to*—has dominated adult thinking for a long time, and it is that very mentality that has caused many people to believe that poor motivation is the driving force behind concerning behaviors. But the research doesn't tell us that your child is lacking motivation. Plus, if that mentality, and the strategies that go along with it, were serving you well, you wouldn't be reading this book right now. There is no great risk in viewing things through different lenses.

So, if you're not focused on behaviors—rewarding the ones you like and punishing the ones you don't like—how will your child's behavior improve? By focusing instead on the expectations your child is having difficulty meeting. I'll be referring to those unmet expectations as *unsolved problems* and, in this book, you're going to learn how to solve them. Solving problems is a task ill-suited to time-outs, stickers, berating, lecturing, ignoring, taking away privileges, sending a child to his room, spanking, and a lot of other things caregivers do with the best of intentions. Once a problem is solved, it doesn't cause concerning behavior anymore.

You might be wondering how you ended up with a child who responds so poorly to problems and frustrations. What caused this? Was it nature or nurture? While it's understandable that you'd be asking those questions, they won't be a major focal point of this book. First, both nature and nurture are *always* implicated when it comes to a child's development. And there are many aspects of nature and nurture that could have affected your child's skills in the domains of flexibility, adaptability, frustration tolerance, emotion regulation, and problem solving. It could be the gene pool, the fact that your child was born two months prematurely, or perhaps exposure to substances in utero. It could also be a difficult temperament, trauma history, brain injury, or seizures. Without being dismissive of the potential impact of any of these factors, the reality is that we can't establish the *cause* of your child's concerning behaviors with great precision. But we can identify the skills your child is lacking and the expectations he is having difficulty meeting (you'll learn how in the next two chapters). Those are things you can actually do something about.

Does your child's psychiatric diagnosis provide you with precise information about his lagging skills and unsolved problems? Not really. While diagnoses—such as ADHD, oppositional-defiant disorder, bipolar disorder, depression, autism spectrum disorder, reactive attachment disorder, disruptive mood dysregulation disorder—can be helpful in some ways (for example, they "validate" that there's something different about your child, they might be necessary to qualify your child for special services, and they might be needed to convince your insurance carrier to pay for mental health services), they don't provide you with information about your child's specific lagging skills and unsolved problems. Diagnoses can also be counterproductive in that they imply that the problem resides solely *within the child* and that it's the *child* who needs to be fixed. And, since diagnoses are simply categories containing lists of *concerning behaviors*, they may not be telling you anything about your child that you didn't already know.

But aren't some concerning behaviors more severe than others? Yes, no doubt. Some kids—the *lucky* ones—cry, pout, sulk, whine, or withdraw when they're struggling with problems and frustrations. They're lucky because caregivers tend to respond to these less severe behaviors in ways that are more supportive, empathic, and nurturing. Other kids—the *unlucky* ones—scream, swear, hit, kick, bite, spit, destroy property, or worse. These behaviors are definitely more severe, and we adults tend to respond to them in ways that are far less empathic and far harsher and more punitive. But whether a child's concerning behavior is lucky or unlucky, it's communicating the exact same thing: *I'm stuck . . . there's an expectation I'm having difficulty meeting.*

Of course, if you're the parent of a kid who is communicating that he's having difficulty meeting expectations in ways that are unlucky, your life is definitely harder. But it's going to stay harder if you're still thinking that your child's behavior is manipulative, attention-seeking, unmotivated, stubborn, willful, intransigent, bratty, spoiled, controlling, resistant, out of control, and defiant.

So, we have some important things to figure out about your child. ***What skills is he lacking?*** The answer to that question will help you understand *why* your child is responding so poorly to problems and frustrations. ***What expectations is he having difficulty meeting?*** That's going to help you know *when* your child exhibits concerning behaviors. If you identify those unsolved problems *proactively*, they become *highly predictable*. And if they're highly predictable, they can be solved *proactively* rather than in the heat of the moment.

• • •

Well, in only a few pages, we just covered some really important territory. Here are the key points of this chapter:

- If your kid *could* be more flexible, handle frustration more adaptively, and solve problems more proficiently, he *would*, because *kids do well if they can.*

- Handling problems and frustrations adaptively requires important skills, ones your child is lacking. It is very important that you come to see your child through the prism of lagging skills rather than lagging motivation.

- Your child's concerning behaviors—whether lucky or unlucky—are communicating that he is having difficulty meeting certain expectations.

- Those expectations—called unsolved problems—are predictable and can be identified and solved proactively.

- The problem-solving process you'll be learning about in a few chapters will not only solve the problems that are causing your child's concerning behaviors, but it will also reduce his concerning behavior and enhance the skills your child is lacking. And it will help you and your child become allies, not adversaries. Partners, not enemies.

Hard to fathom? Understandable. When you've been thinking and parenting in a certain way for a long time, changing lenses and practices can take some doing. You'll learn about these changes in the next few chapters.

• • •

Debbie knocked at the door of Jennifer's bedroom, opening it very slightly. "Jennifer, I'm going to take a walk."

As expected, Jennifer was still watching a movie, wearing headphones. She didn't acknowledge Debbie's announcement.

Debbie opened the door a bit farther—a high-risk move—and raised her voice (another high-risk move). "I'm taking a walk," she said loudly.

Jennifer looked annoyed, paused her movie, and removed one headphone. "Why do you always scream at me?" she groused. But Debbie could sense that, at the moment, the level of agitation wasn't extreme.

"I wasn't screaming. I didn't know if you heard me."

"I heard you. Can I go to the store later? I need a new pair of rain boots. Mine are too small."

"We can try to do that later, yes," said Debbie.

Ambiguity was not Jennifer's strong suit. "Well, can we or can't we?"

"I think we can, but I need to find out what Dad and Riley are doing before I say yes for sure."

"I need rain boots!" Jennifer intoned.

"I know that, Jennifer. I'll do my best."

This response was no less ambiguous, but Jennifer was distracted by her movie and the fuse didn't light. Debbie was tempted to ask Jennifer what movie she was watching but decided instead on a quick escape.

Once outside, Debbie called her friend Sandra. They'd met in a support group a few years back and had talked almost daily since. They often laughed about their unlikely friendship and the fact that they'd come from "different sides of the tracks." Debbie came from a solidly middle-class background, graduated from college, married her high school sweetheart, and had been primed to have the model family (until Jennifer put the kibosh on that game plan). Sandra came from harder circumstances. She was born to a teenage mom whose pregnancy did not interrupt her drug use, never knew her biological father, lived with different relatives at various points of childhood and adolescence, was roughed up on several occasions by her mother's boyfriends, ran away and lived on the streets a few times, became pregnant with Frankie when she was sixteen years old, got her GED at age twenty, and now worked as an aide at a nursing home.

Their common bond was the concerning behavior of their children. Frankie, now thirteen, had episodes that were more severe than Jennifer's and had experienced the "outer edges" of treatment for kids with concerning behaviors (he'd already had multiple placements on inpatient psychiatry units and was in a special education program for kids with emotional and behavioral challenges).

"Hey," Debbie said when Sandra answered. "Do you have a minute?"

"Sure. Just hanging out with Frankie," Sandra said. "He has that bug going around."

"I'm sorry, I'll let you go."

"No, no, he's on the couch watching TV. He's actually rather pleasant when he's sick. Kinda pathetic actually. Makes me wish he was sick all the time."

"You're funny. I feel the same way about Jennifer sometimes. It's the only time she lets me mother her."

"So, what's up?"

Debbie thought it was a little twisted that she looked forward to telling Sandra about Jennifer's latest blow-up—and to hearing Sandra's stories as well—but it made her feel less alone.

"If you can believe it, we had a blowout over waffles this morning."

"Waffles? Why?"

"Well, Jennifer decided that she had the monopoly on the family waffles, and went a little wacko when Riley decided he wanted waffles, too."

"Oh my. Was it ugly?"

"A lot less ugly than it could've been. It's actually sorta comical, now that I'm thinking about it . . . watching her stalk off to her room to protect her waffles. Although Riley and I didn't think it was funny at the time. Poor kid."

"That's why I'm glad I don't have any kids besides Frankie. No one has to suffer besides me."

"I feel bad for Riley," said Debbie. "He's gotten a raw deal in the sibling department. But it's nice to have one child who's well-behaved . . . it helps me know I'm actually capable of raising a well-behaved kid."

"Yeah, well, I'm stuck with just my one out-of-control kid. I'm the stereotypical bad single mom. Just ask his teachers."

"I think you deserve a medal for what you've been through with that kid."

"You showing up at my awards ceremony?"

"I think all parents of challenging kids deserve an award," said Debbie. "Not just for what we live with . . . but for tolerating what people say about us!"

"Did you tell Kevin about the waffle episode?"

"Yeah."

"Did he lose it?"

"Not this time."

"Are you going to tell Jennifer's therapist about it?"

"I already emailed her, but I doubt she'll give me much guidance on what to do. She never does. She just meets with Jennifer and they talk about whatever they talk about and I'm left wondering what I'm supposed to do when she goes nuts and my other kid is petrified and my husband loses his mind. Jennifer doesn't even want to go see her anymore. The only reason I make her go is because I need to feel like I'm doing *something*. Otherwise I'd be doing nothing."

3

LAGGING SKILLS

You already know what concerning behaviors your child exhibits. You may also know what diagnoses have been applied to your child based on those behaviors. And you may have spent some meaningful time contemplating (and maybe even agonizing over) the potential factors that caused those behaviors.

We're not going to be talking about any of those things for the remainder of this book. In this chapter and the next, we're going to focus instead on the information that's been missing: lagging skills and unsolved problems.

Identifying your child's lagging skills will help you achieve a much better understanding of why she responds so poorly to problems and frustrations. It will also help you take your child's concerning behaviors less personally, respond to your child with greater compassion, and better anticipate situations in which she is likely to run into difficulty. And when you identify the expectations your child is having difficulty meeting—again, those unmet expectations are called unsolved problems—you'll know exactly what problems need to be solved to reduce the likelihood of concerning behaviors. This chapter focuses on identifying your child's lagging skills. In the next chapter, we'll turn our attention to unsolved problems.

Below is the instrument we'll be using to identify both. It's called the *Assessment of Lagging Skills & Unsolved Problems (ALSUP)*, and you can find it in an editable/fillable version on the website of the nonprofit I founded, Lives in the Balance (www.livesin thebalance.org).

Your first task in completing this instrument is to check off the lagging skills that seem to apply to your child. No need to obsess over whether to check off a particular lagging skill. If a lagging skill seems to apply to your child, check it off.

For many parents, those lagging skills represent new information. That new information can cause some parents to feel guilty that they weren't aware of something very important about their child. They may also feel regret about the adversarial interactions they've had with the child, driven by inaccurate beliefs about the child's behavior. They wonder why none of

ALSUP 2020
ASSESSMENT OF LAGGING SKILLS & UNSOLVED PROBLEMS

Collaborative & Proactive Solutions
THIS IS HOW PROBLEMS GET SOLVED

CHILD'S NAME _____ DATE _____

The ALSUP is intended for use as a **discussion guide** rather than as a freestanding checklist or rating scale. It should be used to identify specific lagging skills and unsolved problems that pertain to a particular child or adolescent.

LAGGING SKILLS

This section will help you understand why the child is responding so maladaptively to problems and frustrations. Please note that these **lagging skills are not the primary focal point of intervention**. In other words, you won't be discussing the lagging skills with the student, nor will you be teaching most of the skills explicitly. The primary targets of intervention are the unsolved problems you'll be documenting in the next section.

☐	Difficulty maintaining focus	☐	Difficulty seeing "grays"; concrete, literal, black & white thinking
☐	Difficulty handling transitions, shifting from one mindset or task to another	☐	Difficulty taking into account situational factors that would suggest the need to adjust a plan of action
☐	Difficulty considering the likely outcomes or consequences of actions (impulsive)	☐	Inflexible, inaccurate interpretations/cognitive distortions or biases (e.g., "Everyone's out to get me," "Nobody likes me")
☐	Difficulty persisting on challenging or tedious tasks	☐	Difficulty attending to or accurately interpreting social cues/poor perception of social nuances
☐	Difficulty considering a range of solutions to a problem	☐	Difficulty shifting from original idea, plan, or solution
☐	Difficulty expressing concerns, needs, or thoughts in words	☐	Difficulty appreciating how his/her behavior is affecting others
☐	Difficulty managing emotional response to frustration so as to think rationally	☐	Difficulty starting conversations, entering groups, connecting with people/lacking other basic social skills
☐	Chronic irritability and/or anxiety significantly impede capacity for problem-solving or heighten frustration	☐	Difficulty empathizing with others, appreciating another person's perspective or point of view
☐	Sensory/motor difficulties	☐	Difficulty handling unpredictability, ambiguity, uncertainty, novelty

UNSOLVED PROBLEMS

Unsolved problems are the specific expectations a child is having difficulty meeting. The wording of an unsolved problem will translate directly into the words that you'll be using when you introduce an unsolved problem to the child when it comes time to solve the problem together. Poorly worded unsolved problems often cause the problem-solving process to deteriorate before it even gets started. Please reference the ALSUP Guide for guidance on the four guidelines for writing unsolved problems.

SCHOOL/FACILITY PROMPTS:
Are there specific tasks/expectations the student is having difficulty completing or getting started on?
Are there classmates this student is having difficulty getting along with in specific conditions?
Are there tasks and activities this student is having difficulty moving from or to?
Are there classes/activities the student is having difficulty attending/being on time to?

HOME/CLINIC PROMPTS:
Are there chores/tasks/activities the child is having difficulty completing or getting started on?
Are there siblings/other children the child is having difficulty getting along with in specific conditions?
Are there aspects of hygiene the child is having difficulty completing?
Are there activities the child is having difficulty ending or tasks the child is having difficulty moving on to?

LIVES
IN THE
BALANCE

the mental health professionals they've consulted told them about lagging skills and unsolved problems (the reason is probably that the training these professionals received took them in a different direction). And they wonder if it's too late to turn things around and whether their relationship with their child is irretrievably broken.

It's not too late to turn things around, and your relationship with your child is not irretrievably broken.

Some parents feel overwhelmed by the sheer number of lagging skills they've checked off for their child. But those lagging skills have been there all along; good that you now know what they are.

Other parents feel that lagging skills are too negative. Those lagging skills don't diminish your child's many positive attributes, but they do explain why your child has been responding to problems and frustrations so maladaptively. And, compared to many of the other things that have been said about your child, perhaps *accurate* is more apt.

Some caregivers wonder how they're going to teach all of those lagging skills. Well, you don't actually need to teach most of them, not explicitly anyway. *Those skills will be enhanced by solving problems* in the ways you'll soon learn. The primary goal of identifying lagging skills is to ensure that you have the right lenses on. Your child is lacking skills, not motivation.

Just to make sure those new lenses are helping you see things as clearly as possible, let's take some time to think more about how some specific lagging skills would make it difficult for your child to respond to problems and frustrations adaptively. No need to be exhaustive here; just a sampling.

- Difficulty considering a range of solutions to a problem
- Difficulty considering past experiences that would guide one's actions in the present (hindsight)
- Difficulty considering the likely outcomes or consequences of one's solutions or potential courses of action (forethought)

What's the main thing your brain must do when you're faced with a problem? Solve it. That may seem pretty straightforward, but only if you have the skills to accomplish the mission.

Most of us have never given much thought to the actual thinking processes that are involved in solving a problem because we do it fairly automatically, but if you have a kid with concerning behaviors it's definitely worth thinking about because she's not doing it fairly automatically.

First, you need to consider the range of responses or solutions that would help you solve the problem (those solutions are almost always drawn from past experiences). Then you need to think about the likely outcomes of each potential solution so that you can pick the best one. Many kids have great difficulty considering a range of potential solutions that could be applied to a particular problem. Some can't think of any solutions at all. Many also have difficulty anticipating how each potential solution would pan out. Some are so impulsive that, even if they could think of more than one solution, they've already done the first thing that popped into their heads. The bad news is that the first solution is often the worst one, the one that required the *least* amount of reflection and thought, which probably explains why some kids are notorious for putting their worst foot forward. Moreover, there are many kids who can't think of any solutions at all. So, the problem remains unsolved. And the concerning behaviors being caused by that problem persist.

- Difficulty expressing concerns, needs, or thoughts in words

Thank goodness humans learned, way back when, how to communicate using words. Language is what separates us from the other species (other species have language, but not as sophisticated and nuanced as ours). Language is the mechanism by which we exchange information about our thoughts, ideas, concerns, perspectives, and emotions. It's the mechanism by which we *think*. And, though most of us haven't thought about it much, language is the primary way in which we solve problems.

Yes, it's internal language (self-talk) that helps us

navigate and think our way through potential solutions ("I might not even feel like having waffles tomorrow morning . . . plus, I can ask my mom to buy more to-day . . . so it's not such a big deal if my brother eats the rest of the waffles right now . . ."). Many kids lack that skill. Other kids may not have a basic vocabulary for letting people know they "need a break," that "some-thing's the matter," that they "can't talk about that right now," that they "need a minute" to collect their thoughts or shift gears, or that they "don't like that." Since they lack the wherewithal to adaptively commu-nicate their thoughts, ideas, concerns, perspectives, and emotions, they may communicate these things us-ing less optimal words: "screw you," "I hate you," "shut up," and "leave me alone" are some of the milder pos-sibilities. Some kids can't muster any words and growl, scream, or hit instead. Take Gus, for example:

PARENT: Gus, I understand you got pretty frustrated at school today.

GUS: Yup.

PARENT: What happened?

GUS: Sammy wanted to play with my toys, and I didn't want him to.

PARENT: So what did you do?

GUS: I kicked him.

PARENT: You kicked Sammy?

GUS: Yes.

PARENT: What happened next?

GUS: He told on me.

PARENT: And next?

GUS: I got put in time-out.

PARENT: Did that make you mad?

GUS: Yes.

PARENT: Which part made you mad?

GUS: It made me mad that Sammy took my toys.

PARENT: Were you mad about getting put in time-out?

GUS: Kinda. But I'm in time-out a lot, so I'm kinda used to it.

PARENT: Is it OK for you to kick Sammy?

GUS: No.

PARENT: How come you didn't tell Sammy that you didn't want him to play with the toys you were playing with?

GUS: I didn't know what to say.

PARENT: Is this the first time you and Sammy have had this problem with the toys?

GUS: No, Sammy always wants to play with my toys.

If Gus already knows that he shouldn't kick Sammy, then he doesn't need yet another time-out to drive home the point. If what's really going on is that Gus is having trouble coming up with the words to let Sammy know that he's still playing with certain toys, then we'd need to help him solve that problem, something no number of time-outs would accomplish. So long as that problem is unsolved, Gus is going to keep kicking Sammy. If, as Gus suggests, this isn't the first time that Gus and Sammy have had a conflict over sharing toys, then this is a highly predictable unsolved problem and it can be solved proactively. Even if that problem has never come up before, it's predictable now (because it's already happened once).

- Difficulty regulating emotions

As you know, solving problems is much easier if a person has the ability to think through solutions. But frustration, anxiety, and other strong emotions can make the thinking part a lot harder. It's not that the emotions are all bad: mild emotions can be useful for mobilizing or energizing people to solve a problem. It's the really strong emotions that get in the way. So, the skill of putting one's emotions on the shelf so as to think through solutions to problems more objectively, rationally, and logically—a skill called *separation of affect*—is really important. Kids who are pretty good at this skill tend to respond to problems or frustrations with more thought than emotion, and that's good. But children whose skills in this domain are lacking tend to respond to problems or frustrations with less thought and more emotion, and that's not so good. They often aren't able to stem the emotional tide until later, when the emotions have subsided and rational thought has kicked back in. Then they're often remorseful for what happened when they were upset. They may even have the knowledge to deal successfully with problems and can actually demonstrate such knowledge under calmer circumstances, but at the moment they're emotionally aroused, their powerful emotions prevent them from accessing and using the information. You know what this looks like:

PARENT: Philip, come eat the scrambled eggs I made for breakfast.

PHILIP (responding with more emotion than thought, but also telling the truth): I hate scrambled eggs! You always make things I don't like!

PARENT: Well, that's what I made your sister! I made enough for both of you!

PHILIP: Well, that's not what I want!

PARENT: I'm not running a restaurant! And I'm not sending you to school on an empty stomach! Eat the eggs!

PHILIP (dumping the eggs in the sink): No, I hate eggs!

PARENT (now perhaps also responding with more emotion than thought): Your Xbox is history, pal!

PHILIP: [kaboom]

So far, we've only been talking about in-the-moment emotion regulation. But there are some kids whose difficulties in managing emotions are more chronic. In other words, there are kids who are irritable, agitated, cranky, and/or fatigued much more often and much more intensely than others are. Most of us have more trouble handling frustration and solving problems when we're in a bad mood. But these kids are in a bad mood a lot, so they have trouble handling frustration and solving problems a lot, too:

MOTHER: Mickey, why so grumpy? It's a beautiful day outside. Why are you indoors?

MICKEY (slumped in a chair, agitated): It's windy.

MOTHER: It's windy?

MICKEY (more agitated): I said it's windy! I hate wind!

MOTHER: Mickey, you could be out playing basketball, swimming . . . you're this upset over a little wind?

MICKEY (very agitated): It's too windy, damn it! Leave me alone!

MOTHER: Should we try to think of something you could do instead?

MICKEY: There's nothing else to do instead.

Because it can get in the way of rational thought, anxiety can have the same effect as irritability. Again, a little anxiety can actually be helpful, for it can spur a person to take action. But too much anxiety can make rational thinking much harder, which only makes the person more anxious.

- Difficulty seeing the "grays"; concrete, literal, black-and-white thinking
- Difficulty deviating from rules or routine
- Difficulty handling unpredictability, ambiguity, uncertainty, or novelty

- Difficulty shifting from original idea or solution
- Difficulty adapting to changes in plan or new rules
- Difficulty taking into account situational factors that would suggest the need to adjust a plan

Very young children tend to be fairly rigid, black-and-white, literal thinkers. That's because they're still making sense of the world and it's easier to put two and two together if you don't have to worry about exceptions to the rules or alternative ways of looking at things. As children develop, they learn that, in fact, most things in life are "gray"; there *are* exceptions to the rules and alternative ways of interpreting things. We don't go home from grandma's house the same way every time; we don't eat dinner at the exact same time every day; and the weather doesn't always cooperate with our plans.

Unfortunately, for some children, "gray" thinking doesn't develop readily. These are the kids who sometimes end up with diagnoses on the autism spectrum, but regardless of diagnosis they're best thought of as *black-and-white thinkers living in a gray world*. They often have significant difficulty approaching the world in a flexible, adaptable way and become extremely frustrated when events don't proceed in the manner they had originally conceived.

More specifically, these children often have a strong preference for predictability and routines, and struggle when events are unpredictable, uncertain, and ambiguous. These are the kids who run into trouble when they need to adjust or reconfigure their expectations, the ones who tend to overfocus on facts and details and who often have trouble recognizing the obvious or "seeing the big picture." For example, a child may insist on going out for recess at a certain time on a given day because it is the time the class always goes out for recess, failing to take into account both the likely consequences of insisting on the original plan of action (e.g., being at recess alone) and important situational factors (an assembly, perhaps) that would suggest the need for an adaptation of the plan. These children may experience enormous frustration as they struggle to apply concrete rules to a world where few such rules apply:

PARENT: Courtney, we can't go to the park today . . . it's raining.

COURTNEY: But we were supposed to go to the park!

PARENT: I know . . . I wish it wasn't raining, but I don't really see how we can still go . . . we'd get all wet.

COURTNEY: No, we still have to go to the park! That's the plan!

PARENT: We can always go tomorrow if the weather's nicer.

COURTNEY: We're supposed to go today!

PARENT: How 'bout we go to a movie instead?

COURTNEY: No! We're supposed to go to the park!

PARENT: Look, Courtney, it's raining. We'd get all wet.
I'm not going to the park in the pouring rain!
COURTNEY: [kaboom]

After the storm passes, the parent might try asking
the usual:

PARENT: Courtney, how come you got so upset when
we couldn't go to the park because of the rain?
COURTNEY: I don't know.

That's actually a pretty informative response,
though it may not seem like it. In a perfect world, the
child would respond with something like "See, guys, I
have a little problem. Actually, it's a pretty big problem. I'm not very good at being flexible, handling frustration, and solving problems. And you—and lots of
other people—expect me to handle changes in plans
and things not going the way I thought they would
with great ease. When you expect these things, I start
to get frustrated, and then I have trouble thinking
clearly, and then I get even more frustrated. Then you
guys get frustrated, and that just makes it worse. Then
I start doing things I wish I didn't do and saying things
I wish I didn't say. Then you sometimes do things you
wish you didn't do and say things you wish you didn't
say. Then you punish me, and it gets really messy. After the dust settles—you know, when I start thinking
clearly again—I end up being really sorry for the things

I did and said. I know this isn't fun for you, but rest assured, I'm not having any fun either."

These kids are rarely able to describe their difficulties with this kind of clarity. But here's a simple math equation that might suffice.

INFLEXIBILITY + INFLEXIBILITY = MELTDOWN

Hopefully, if it wasn't already, the connection between lagging skills and maladaptive responses to problems and frustrations is now clear. Just to make sure, let's take a close look—just for a few pages—at some of the inaccurate things that have been said about your child so we can put them to rest once and for all.

She Just Wants Attention

This common cliché is often invoked to explain why kids are exhibiting concerning behavior. But we *all* just want attention, so that doesn't really distinguish your child from anyone else. If your child had the skills to seek attention adaptively, she would. More importantly, what's the logical intervention for a kid who we think is seeking attention maladaptively? Ignore her, so as to deprive her of the attention she's seeking. But if her concerning behavior is instead communicating that she's having difficulty meeting a particular expectation, then simply ignoring the behavior will cause us to miss the boat on what's really getting in the way.

She's Manipulating Us

Here we have another popular but misguided way of portraying kids with concerning behaviors. Competent manipulation requires various skills—forethought, planning, impulse control, organization—that, as you've read, are typically found lacking in kids with concerning behaviors.

She's Not Motivated

Once you've identified a kid's lagging skills and unsolved problems, "unmotivated" no longer makes sense as an explanation for the kid's concerning behaviors. *Kids do well if they can*, so she's motivated already.

She's Making Bad Choices

She's choosing to exhibit concerning behaviors instead of adaptive behaviors? Why would she do that? Her life would be a lot better if she had the skills to make good choices.

She Has a Bad Attitude

She probably didn't start out with one. "Bad attitudes" tend to be the by-product of countless years of being misunderstood, overcorrected, overdirected, and overpunished by adults who didn't recognize that a kid lacked crucial thinking skills. But kids are resilient; they come around if we start doing the right thing.

She Knows Just What Buttons to Push

We should reword this one so it's more accurate: *when she's having difficulty meeting certain expectations, she exhibits concerning behaviors that adults experience as being extremely unpleasant.*

She Has a Mental Illness

You mean that she meets diagnostic criteria for a psychiatric disorder? As you've read, that just tells us what concerning behaviors she exhibits when she's having difficulty meeting certain expectations. Borrowing from a renowned psychologist, Thomas Szasz, the term *problems in living* is far preferable to the term *mental illness*, for it points us in the direction of what really needs to be done to help kids with concerning behaviors: solve the problems that are causing those behaviors.

By the way, there's a big difference between interpreting lagging skills as *excuses* rather than as *explanations*. When lagging skills are invoked as excuses, the door slams shut on the process of thinking about how to help a child. Conversely, when lagging skills are used as explanations for why a child responds so poorly to problems and frustrations, the door to helping the child swings wide open and caregivers are freed up to consider alternative strategies for helping.

• • •

Here is a summary of the important points of this chapter:

- A variety of lagging skills can make it difficult for a kid to respond to life's problems and frustrations in an adaptive, rational manner.

- Identifying your child's lagging skills can help you understand her difficulties more accurately, take her concerning behaviors less personally, and respond in ways that are more compassionate, less punitive, and more effective.

- Those lagging skills should also change your vocabulary. Attention-seeking, manipulative, unmotivated, and so forth . . . these characterizations of your child were never accurate and simply perpetuate the use of interventions that may not have been serving your child—and you—well at all.

• • •

Kevin was watching a football game with Riley when Debbie burst into the living room. "Honey, you need to come see this!" she said.

"What'd she do now?" Kevin groused, certain that Jennifer was refusing to do something.

"I found something on the web . . . you need to see it!" Debbie implored.

Relieved that there was no crisis at the moment, Kevin's attention turned back to the television. "I'm watching the game with Riley."

"This is important."

"Watching the game with Riley is important."

"Please."

"Will it still be there at half-time? This is, like, the only thing I do to relax."

Like I do anything to relax, thought Debbie, quickly cognizant that some things are best left unsaid. "So, screaming at the quarterback is relaxing? Fine, come to the computer at half-time."

When Kevin came over to the computer, Debbie was engrossed in a video. "You're all worked up over a video?"

"Listen to this." Debbie went back to the beginning of the video.

Kevin watched the speaker in the video talking about kids with concerning behaviors. He was saying that the child's behavior was not the most important part of the picture. "What a fruitcake," Kevin groused. "He should live in my house for five minutes . . . we'll see if he thinks the behavior is important then."

"Just listen," said Debbie.

The speaker was also saying that instead of putting their energy into rewarding and punishing behavior, adults should instead focus on solving the problems giving rise to those behaviors.

Kevin was confused. "Problems?"

"Yes, problems!" said Debbie. "The stuff we fight with her about all the time! Going to bed at night . . . taking a shower . . . getting up in the morning . . . homework . . . *problems*! And *solving* them . . . but not the way we're doing it now! And he says she acts the way she does because she's lacking *skills*!"

Kevin didn't completely understand, and he was skeptical. His wife spent a lot of time surfing the web, reading blogs and books and magazines, and watching TV shows—anything that might help her with Jennifer. "Just what we need, another doctor making a lot of money on getting saps like us to buy stuff that doesn't really work."

"The stuff on this website is free."

"Nothing is free. What's he selling?"

"I haven't noticed that he's selling anything. He has ideas I haven't heard before. And they make sense."

"I'm glad they make sense. Can I go back and watch my game now?"

"This is about our daughter."

"I spend half of my life thinking about our daughter. You spend your *whole* life thinking about our daughter. And I really want to watch my game! Where is she, by the way?"

"She's watching a movie in her bedroom."

"I knew it was quiet around here. When the movie's over

and she's going nuts about something, maybe you should track down the doctor in the video so he can help us deal with it. Did he give you his phone number?"

"That doctor says that by the time she's going nuts it's already too late."

"Too late . . ." Kevin's mind was already elsewhere. "Can I watch my game . . . before I'm too late for the second half?"

"Fine, go watch your game, scream at the television, relax. But I think this guy is on to something." Debbie turned back to her computer screen.

4

UNSOLVED PROBLEMS

Let's now turn our attention to *when* your child is exhibiting concerning behaviors. The key to reducing those behaviors is to solve the problems that are causing them, so identifying your child's unsolved problems is essential.

Many caregivers believe that a kid's concerning behaviors are unpredictable and occur "out of the blue." That may explain why they wait until concerning behaviors "pop up" (yet again) before they try to deal with them (yet again). But most kids with concerning behaviors are reliably set off by the same five or six (or ten or twelve) problems every day or every week. In other words, unsolved problems are *predictable*—they don't really "pop up"—so they can be solved *proactively*. A very important goal of this book is to get you out of the heat of the moment. You want to be in crisis *prevention* mode, not crisis *management* mode.

While most parents have no difficulty chronicling their child's concerning behaviors, pinpointing the problems that are causing those behaviors can be more of a challenge. Remember, unsolved problems are expectations your child is having difficulty meeting. If you expect your child to take out the trash on Tuesday mornings, and they're not reliably meeting that expectation, then that's an unsolved problem. If you expect your child to be in bed by 8:30 pm, and they're not reliably meeting that expectation, that's an unsolved problem. If you expect your child to be home by a 12 am curfew, and they're not reliably meeting that expectation, that's an unsolved problem.

Identifying unsolved problems is a little harder than checking off lagging skills, especially because you'll want to be very precise in your wording. That's because **the wording of the unsolved problem on the ALSUP is going to translate directly into the words you use when you introduce the unsolved problem to your child when it comes time to solve it.** Poorly worded unsolved problems often cause the problem-solving process to come to an immediate halt before it even gets started. So, there are a few guidelines you'll want to keep in mind. The guidelines aren't there to make things harder (though it may seem that way at first); they're there to make it more likely that your child will participate in the problem-solving process.

GUIDELINE #1: The wording of unsolved problems should contain no mention of your child's concerning behavior. In other words, you wouldn't write, "Gets upset and kicks brother when having difficulty sharing toys in the playroom." Instead, start your unsolved problems with the word *difficulty* and get rid of the concerning behavior altogether: "Difficulty sharing toys with brother in the playroom."

Why is it important to leave the concerning behavior out of the wording of the unsolved problem? Because many kids become defensive and won't participate in the problem-solving process if you highlight their concerning behavior at the beginning of that process. And having your child participate in the problem-solving process is really important.

By the way, what almost always comes after the word *difficulty* is a verb. For example:

- Difficulty *waking up* for school by 7 am

- Difficulty *completing* the algebra worksheet for homework

- Difficulty *emptying* the dishwasher

- Difficulty *getting started* on the word problems worksheet for homework

- Difficulty *ending* the Xbox game to come in for dinner

- Difficulty *putting away* clean laundry

GUIDELINE #2: The wording of the unsolved problem should contain no adult theories. You wouldn't write "Difficulty completing the paragraphs on the Language Arts homework because she just doesn't feel like doing them" because "she just doesn't feel like doing them" is your theory. Follow this rule of thumb: the minute you're inclined to write the word *because* in the unsolved problem, stop writing. Everything that comes after *because* is a theory.

Why is it important to jettison your theories? First, because adult theories about the cause of an unsolved problem are often incorrect. In other words, there's a decent chance that what you *thought* was making it difficult for your child to meet a particular expectation is *not* what is actually making it difficult for your child to meet that expectation. Second, including a theory in the wording of an unsolved problem could make it harder for your kid to think about and tell you what's making it hard to meet a particular expectation. It's not your job to know what's hard; it's your job to know how to find out. **Your child is your best source on what's making it difficult for them to meet a given expectation.** Even if your child is a reluctant talker. Even if your child is nonspeaking.

GUIDELINE #3: Make sure the unsolved problems are "split" rather than "clumped." Here's an example of a *clumped* unsolved problem: *Difficulty completing homework.* If your child is having difficulty completing *many* different homework assignments, then clumping the wording of that unsolved problem will make it more difficult for your child to provide information about what's hard about *any* of them. So, if your child is having difficulty writing the paragraphs on the Language Arts homework and also having difficulty completing the worksheet on Ponce de Leon, then those are two separate unsolved problems (even though they're both homework assignments). And if they're also having difficulty memorizing their multiplication tables, then that's a separate unsolved problem, too.

Is this guideline going to make your list of unsolved problems very long? Yes, probably. But at least now you know what those unsolved problems are so you can get on with the business of solving them. Isn't a long list of unsolved problems a bit overwhelming? Yes, coming to an awareness of the sheer number of expectations your child is having difficulty meeting can be a bit jarring. But if that helps you reconsider whether your child can actually meet all those expectations, that would be a good thing. And you're not going to be solving all of them at once.

• • •

A few nights later, after Jennifer and Riley were in bed, Debbie and Kevin sat down together at the kitchen table. Debbie had printed out two copies of the ALSUP that she had found on the website. Their goal: to identify Jennifer's lagging skills and unsolved problems.

"Now, we're supposed to identify her lagging skills first," explained Debbie. "So, we just check it off if it applies to Jennifer."

Kevin began scanning his copy of the ALSUP. "Why are we doing this?"

"Because after all these years, we still don't know why Jennifer gets so upset so often and so easily," said Debbie.

Kevin sighed. "And we can figure this out on our own?"

"It's not like any of the doctors we've seen have nailed it," said Debbie.

"And this sheet of paper is going to tell us?"

"Yes," said Debbie. "And by the way, I already looked at the list of lagging skills, and she basically lights up the board."

"You started without me?" said Kevin, feigning insult.

"I start everything without you." Debbie smiled.

Kevin looked at his copy of the ALSUP. "Where do we put stuff like hitting, and screaming, and swearing?"

"We don't," said Debbie. "Those are the things she's doing *because* of her lagging skills and unsolved problems."

"Hitting seems like a pretty big problem to me," said Kevin.

"Yeah, but that's not what we're going to be working on with Jennifer," said Debbie. "That's the whole point. All these years we've been focused on her *behavior*, when we should have been focused on solving the problems that *cause* her behavior."

"I'm not going to let her hit people," said Kevin.

"I understand we're not going to let her hit people," said Debbie, trying to stay patient. "But we're going to get rid of the hitting by solving the problems that are causing her to get upset."

"Jennifer's always getting upset," said Kevin.

"Yeah, that's what I thought at first," said Debbie. "But she's not always getting upset. We have to be more specific about when she's getting upset. Otherwise, we won't know what problems we're trying to solve with her. Can we just start? What about this first lagging skill? 'Difficulty making transitions.' What do you think?"

"I think that one's true," said Kevin.

"I agree," said Debbie. "So, I'm going to check it off. Let's decide which of these other lagging skills apply to her."

They checked off fifteen of the eighteen lagging skills.

"Geez, she's lacking a lot of skills," said Kevin, looking a bit unsettled.

"Kinda eye-opening, yes?" said Debbie. "Shall we identify the unsolved problems now?" Kevin tackled this task with greater fervor.

Here's a partial list of the unsolved problems they identified:

- Difficulty eating dinner at the dinner table with family

- Difficulty eating what mom makes for dinner

- Difficulty eating foods besides waffles for breakfast

- Difficulty turning off video when it's time to go to church

- Difficulty agreeing with Riley on what TV show to watch when watching TV together

- Difficulty discussing what restaurant to eat at when the family is going out for dinner

- Difficulty participating in family movie night

- Difficulty completing the Shakespeare worksheet for homework

- Difficulty being in bed with the lights out by 9 pm

- Difficulty going to church on Sunday morning

- Difficulty going to Grandma's house

- Difficulty finding a friend to hang out with on weekends

Notice—you may not need this reminder by now, but just in case—that *hitting* and *screaming* and *swearing* are not included in the wording of the unsolved problems. Again, that's because those are concerning *behaviors* and the word *difficulty* has taken their place.

• • •

"This isn't so hard," said Kevin.

"Nope, not hard at all. We should have done this ten years ago."

"How come we didn't figure this stuff out before?"

"Because we didn't know what we didn't know," said Debbie.

"She has a lot of unsolved problems," Kevin observed soberly.

"And all this time, we could have been busy solving them! But that's not what we've been doing! We've been getting her diagnosed, and giving her stickers, and punishing her, and yelling at her. We've been spinning our wheels!"

"It's kind of sad that we didn't know this stuff about our own daughter."

"Sad for us and sad for her," said Debbie.

"And don't forget about Riley," said Kevin. "So, all those diagnoses she has . . . they don't mean anything?"

"They certainly didn't help me understand Jennifer as well as the lagging skills and unsolved problems do," said Debbie.

"But how are we going to solve all the problems once we know what they are?"

"Let's stay focused here," said Debbie. "That comes next."

• • •

Frankie was playing a video game in his bedroom. Sandra paced in the living room, smoldering. After missing several days of school because of the flu, Frankie had been suspended that day—his first day back—for swearing at a teacher.

They told me they knew how to handle kids like Frankie, Sandra fumed. *He promised to try as hard as he could to stay out of trouble. Now he's blowing it, again. And after only a month!*

Anger had been a familiar companion since Sandra was a kid. Back then, it wasn't just her circumstances that fueled her anger, it was also the sense that she could do very little to change those circumstances. The anger had always energized her to fight harder. But the anger and determination always seemed to backfire in her interactions with Frankie; it just caused him to fight back.

His new school program had given her hope that maybe a corner had been turned. Now this. As she was in the midst of getting her bearings on whether to cry or scream, her phone rang.

It was Debbie, who immediately deciphered Sandra's agitation. "What happened?" asked Debbie with foreboding.

"Frankie got suspended from school today."

"I'm sorry. I guess he's over the flu."

"Oh, he seems to be back in full force."

"Did you have to miss work?"

"I had to leave work to pick him up. My boss said I can't keep doing this." Sandra tried to keep her voice from trembling. "How the heck am I supposed to make this work?"

"I'm sorry," said Debbie.

"It's a freaking special education program! They're supposed to be able to handle him! What are they sending him home for?"

"Makes no sense," said Debbie, trying to empathize.

"And I don't even know what happened! All I know is he swore at someone. What am I supposed to do about it?! I wasn't there! This always happens. He does well for a while, then he screws it up."

"What are you going to do?"

"They want me to come to a meeting tomorrow. I have to miss work for that, too. I swear he's going to get me fired. Then we won't have a place to live either."

"I'm sorry," Debbie said again.

Sandra took a deep breath, exhaling slowly. "So, help me decide who to scream at," she said, only half joking.

"Who are the candidates?" asked Debbie.

"My son, for starters. But if I scream at him, he'll scream back, and it'll get ugly and that never accomplishes anything."

"OK, so cross him off your list. Who else?"

"Do we have to cross him off the list so fast?" asked Sandra, half joking again. "I cannot tell you how tired I am of dealing with this crap."

"I know," said Debbie. "Who else could you scream at?"

"The director of his program at school. But that's pointless, too. He'll just think I'm a crazy mom who's overprotective of her kid and doesn't understand why he had to suspend him. Been there, done that."

"Probably worth crossing him off your list, too. Any others?"

"That's pretty much it. Guess I'm not screaming at anybody."

"You can scream at me a little if it would help."

Sandra laughed. "I think I did that already. Sorry."

"You've been dealing with things going badly at school for a long time." Debbie reflected on the process she and Kevin had just gone through with the ALSUP. "Too bad they're not focused on his lagging skills and unsolved problems."

"His what?"

"I found this website . . ." Debbie paused. "You know what, this might not be the best time."

"Lay it on me, honey. I need a diversion."

"Are you sure you want to hear about it right now?"

"No time like the present. Is it going to keep my kid in school?"

"Um, I don't know. But I thought it was pretty informative. It helped us learn things about Jennifer that we didn't know."

"Oh, I think I know Frankie pretty well. He hits, he screams, he swears, he gets thrown out of school . . ."

"Well, that's just it," said Debbie. "According to this website, those behaviors aren't the most important thing about Frankie."

"They seem pretty important to the people who are throwing him out of school," said Sandra, unconvinced.

"I know. But the important part is *why* he's doing those things."

"He's doing those things because he's bipolar. You know that," said Sandra.

"Bipolar disorder is just his diagnosis," said Debbie. "But it's not why he does that stuff."

"And this website is going to tell me why?"

"Yeah, and what to do about it," said Debbie.

"Oh, I don't think there's anything anybody can do about it," said Sandra, even more dubious. "He's been on every medicine known to mankind. He's pretty severe."

"Yeah, but part of the reason he's pretty severe is because no one's ever figured out what's really going on with him," said Debbie. "There's this form on the website that's really eye-opening. It helped us understand Jennifer better, and it helped us nail down the problems that get her upset."

"Geez, you're really pumped up."

"All I know is, it's the first time Kevin and I have been on the same page about anything related to Jennifer. It makes it obvious why all the stuff we've been doing hasn't worked. We've been focused on the wrong things! You really need to fill out the form!"

"OK, I'll check it out. But I'm not getting my hopes up," said Sandra.

Debbie paused. "OK, so don't get your hopes up. But check out the website."

Sandra was too tired and angry to do anything that night. A few nights later, she looked at the ALSUP on the website, but became a little confused when she tried to identify Frankie's unsolved problems and called Debbie.

"I tried filling out the ALSUP," said Sandra.

"Good for you!" said Debbie. "Well?"

"I didn't get very far." .

"How come?"

"Well, the lagging skills were easy enough to check off. But I couldn't quite figure out the unsolved problems."

"We had trouble with that, too. It's easier to think of the behaviors than the problems that are causing them."

"Exactly! How'd you do it?"

"Well, I'm no expert of course, but every time I thought of a behavior, I thought of the situations in which the behavior occurs. The situation is the unsolved problem."

"So, like screaming. Frankie screams all the time."

"What's he screaming about?" asked Debbie.

"Everything."

"Yeah, but *what* exactly? What's an example of something he screams about?"

"He's screaming because I want him to turn down the volume on his music."

"He doesn't have earbuds?"

"No, he's always losing them. He screams about that, too."

"Those are good ones."

"Good what?"

"Good unsolved problems," said Debbie. "All you have to do is try wording them with the word 'difficulty' in front. So, like, 'Difficulty keeping track of his earbuds' would be one. And 'Difficulty keeping his music at a reasonable volume' might be one, too."

"I think I get it," said Sandra. "So, he's going to have a ton of problems, isn't he? I mean, he screams about a lot of things."

"Jennifer had thirty-five unsolved problems. The good part is that once you identify the problems you can start solving them. That's what we should have been doing all along."

"So, have you tried solving any problems yet?" asked Sandra.

"Not yet . . . we might give it a go tonight. Say, what happened at the school meeting?"

"They're not throwing him out of the program yet," said Sandra. "They just wanted to send him a message."

"A message?"

"Yeah, a message. Like he needs more messages. The only message they're sending him is that there's one more place he doesn't belong."

Here's a partial list of the unsolved problems Sandra identified for Frankie:

- Difficulty playing music in the apartment at a reasonable volume

- Difficulty keeping track of earbuds

- Difficulty completing the geography worksheets for homework

- Difficulty completing the double-digit division problems on the math worksheet for homework

- Difficulty reading the assigned passages from *To Kill a Mockingbird* for homework

- Difficulty keeping room clean

- Difficulty putting clothes in laundry hamper

- Difficulty waking up for school in the morning at 7

- Difficulty getting ready for school in time to catch the bus at 7:45 am

- Difficulty coming straight home from school

PRIORITIZING

One last thing before this chapter ends. As you've already read, while a long list of unsolved problems can be overwhelming, you're not going to be trying to solve all of them at once. In fact, trying to solve all the problems at the same time is a very reliable way to ensure that none get solved at all. So, you're going to need to do some prioritizing. You'll need to decide which of your unsolved problems are high priorities and which ones are lower priorities. Your top priority is safety, so any unsolved problems that are setting in motion unsafe behaviors should be a high priority. Unsolved problems that are setting in motion concerning behaviors with great frequency could be high priorities as well. And unsolved problems that are having the greatest negative impact on your child's life or the lives of others could also be prioritized.

So, once you've identified your child's unsolved problems, prioritize your top three. Those will be the ones you start trying to solve first. The rest will end up on the back burner for now.

The back burner? Isn't that giving in?

No, it's not giving in.

Isn't that giving up?

No, it's not that either. It's the recognition that a lot of unsolved problems have piled up over the years and that they aren't going to be solved in one fell swoop.

You're now only one chapter away from learning about how to solve the problems you've prioritized and put the rest on the back burner. But we're going to spend one more chapter thinking about why the strategies you've probably tried already haven't worked and may even have made things worse.

5

THE TRUTH ABOUT CONSEQUENCES

For a very long time, the prevailing view—we'll call it the conventional wisdom—of the cause of concerning behavior in kids has gone something like this: somewhere along the line, kids with concerning behavior *learned* that those behaviors bring them attention or help them get their way by convincing their parents to "give in." A common corollary to this belief is that concerning behavior is planned, intentional, and purposeful (*"He knows exactly what he's doing! He knows what buttons to push!"*). According to the conventional wisdom, how did the child learn these things? He learned them because his parents are passive, permissive, inconsistent, inept disciplinarians (*"What that kid needs are parents who won't back down and make sure he knows who's the boss!"*). Parents who become convinced of this often blame themselves for their child's concerning behaviors (*"We must be doing something wrong!"*). Finally, if you believe that these behaviors are learned and are the result of poor parenting and lax discipline, then it follows that they can also be *un*-learned with better parenting and tighter discipline.

In general, the quest for better parenting and tighter discipline includes the following components:

1. Providing the kid with lots of positive attention for good behavior and eliminating all attention associated with concerning behavior (so as to reduce the likelihood that he will seek attention by exhibiting concerning behavior)

2. Issuing clearer commands

3. Letting kids know that compliance is expected and enforced on all parental commands and that he must comply quickly because his parents are going to issue a command only once or twice

4. Maintaining a record-keeping and currency system (points, stickers, checks, happy faces) to track the child's performance on specified behavioral goals

5. Delivering adult-imposed consequences, in the form of rewards (such as allowance money and privileges), loss of attention (in the form of ignoring and time-out), and punishments (such

as loss of privileges and grounding) contingent
on the child's successful or unsuccessful performance
6. Convincing the child that his parents won't give
in or back down in the face of concerning behavior

At first glance, these components seem pretty reasonable, yes? But let's consider each ingredient and
why you'd want to look before you leap:

1. Your child's concerning behaviors are not for the
purpose of seeking attention. As you've read,
those behaviors simply indicate that your child
is having difficulty meeting certain expectations. If you ignore that—because you're trying
to deprive your child of negative attention—
you'll deprive yourself of the opportunity to
learn more about what's hard for your child and
of the opportunity to solve the problem.
2. If your child is unclear about your expectations,
then issuing clearer commands would be a
great idea. But the vast majority of kids with
concerning behaviors are well aware of their
parents' expectations and equally clear about
how they're expected to behave. Lack of clarity
isn't what's getting in the way.
3. It's fine for you to expect compliance from
your child, and you're already getting compli-

ance on the expectations he's having no difficulty meeting. Demanding rapid compliance
with expectations your child is having difficulty
meeting—and adding adult-imposed consequences to the mix—just throws fuel on the
fire.

4. It's not a tragedy for you to track your child's
progress on specific goals, but if you're tracking
behavior then you're making it quite clear that
you're focused solely on your child's signals, not
on solving the problems that are causing those
signals.

5. Adult-imposed consequences—whether rewards or punishments—are well-suited to
ensuring that your child is motivated to do
well. But if *kids do well if they can*, then your
child is already motivated. The vast majority
of kids I've worked with over the years had
already endured more than their fair share of
consequences. If all those consequences were
going to work, they would have worked a long
time ago.

6. You only need to worry about giving in or back-
ing down if you're engaged in a power struggle.
If you're solving problems with your child, there
is no power struggle.

Why have Debbie and Kevin—and countless other
parents—endured hundreds of outbursts? Because the

guidance they received was based on the conventional wisdom. So, when they gave Jennifer a directive—for example, "Jennifer, it's time to turn off the TV and come in for dinner"—and Jennifer wouldn't budge, they would repeat the directive. Jennifer would (predictably) become frustrated. The parents would then calmly remind Jennifer of the rewards she would receive if she complied and of what would happen (punishment, time-out) if she failed to comply. Jennifer, who badly wanted the rewards and found time-outs and punishments to be decidedly unpleasant, would begin screaming. Debbie and Kevin would interpret Jennifer's increased intensity and failure to respond to their directive as an attempt to force them to back down or give in and would inform her that a time-out was imminent. Jennifer would begin throwing things at her parents. Debbie and Kevin would take Jennifer by the arm to escort her to time-out, an action that would intensify her frustration and irrationality even further. Jennifer would resist being placed in time-out and would try to scratch and claw her parents. They would try to restrain her physically in time-out (many clinicians no longer recommend this practice, but Jennifer's wasn't one of them); Jennifer would (predictably) try to spit on or bite or head-butt them. They would lock Jennifer in her room until she calmed down. Ten minutes to two hours later, Jennifer would stop screaming and swearing. When Jennifer would finally emerge from her room, she was often

QUESTION: So, I'll still be in charge?

ANSWER: You're going to feel a lot more in charge than you do now.

QUESTION: What about natural consequences?

ANSWER: Natural consequences aren't all that different from adult-imposed consequences. Both adult-imposed consequences (e.g., stickers, time-outs, losing privileges) and natural consequences (e.g., if you don't share your toys with your friend, he won't want to play with you; if you touch the hot stove, you'll get burned) are very powerful and very persuasive. Both types of consequences teach kids how you want them to behave and motivate them to behave adaptively. But if a kid is lacking skills rather than motivation, and if the kid already *knows* how you want him to behave, then neither type of consequence is going to get you very far. Again, the vast majority of kids with concerning behaviors I've worked with over the years had already endured more adult-imposed and natural consequences than most of us will experience in our lifetimes. If all those consequences were going to work, they would have worked a long time ago.

• • •

We covered a lot of territory in this chapter; here's a summary of the key points:

- A common belief about kids with concerning behaviors is that they have learned that their concerning behavior is an effective means of getting their
  way and coercing adults into giving in, and that
  their parents are passive, permissive, inconsistent
  disciplinarians.

- This belief has led countless parents to implement
  incentive programs aimed at modifying children's behavior. But such programs don't solve the problems
  that are causing concerning behaviors, and many kids
  and families do not benefit from such programs.

- Your new approach will be focused on solving problems rather than modifying behavior, as you shall see.

• • •

Sandra didn't love doing laundry, but the relative solitude of the
Laundromat gave her time to think. She was still mulling Frankie's latest suspension. She'd tried talking with him about it, but
he'd told her to leave him alone and they'd ended up screaming
at each other instead.

How did it get this bad? She thought back to how awful her
life had been before she became pregnant with Frankie; how the
guy who'd let her move in with him (in exchange for certain benefits) had kicked her out of his apartment when he learned she
was pregnant; how happy she felt to have a kid of her own, even

at the age of sixteen, a kid she was determined to treat way better than her own mom had treated her. Despite spending time in a homeless shelter with her young son, despite not having a reliable income, they'd managed. They had fun together. Frankie was her total focus. She took good care of him. She even stayed out of romantic relationships because she didn't want anything to get in the way of her raising her son. She made sure Frankie knew she expected big things from him, that she wanted him to make something of himself. He seemed really smart to her. *We were pals back then*, she recalled.

Things didn't start deteriorating until Frankie started having difficulties at school in first grade. She began hearing about Frankie being hyperactive and aggressive and about the difficulties he'd begun experiencing on various academic tasks. Frankie received extra help for his learning challenges, but for his behavioral challenges he was kept in from recess, held after school, and began receiving suspensions. Various medications were tried; some made things worse, others had side effects that Frankie couldn't tolerate.

Sandra responded to Frankie's difficulties with the same determination that had seen her through other adversities, but her efforts to encourage her son to behave himself in school only led to screaming matches. Various counselors guided her on using sticker charts and time-outs to deal with Frankie's concerning behaviors. He liked the idea of earning rewards in the beginning, but he became aggressive if he didn't get a reward he was hoping for and eventually lost interest. Time-out wasn't a viable option; Frankie would scream and swear, and the neighbors would complain. Eventually, Frankie refused to talk with Sandra about school; if she broached the subject, he'd become violent—so violent that he'd twice been placed on in-patient psychiatry units. Having seen kids being pinned to the ground and placed in seclusion rooms when they were out of control, Frankie had vowed to run away from home before he'd let himself be put in one of those places again.

Now Frankie and Sandra rarely talked to each other about much of anything. Her thoughts turned to their new home-based mental health counselor, a guy named Matt. Their old counselor—Frankie liked her—had been transferred to another office. The new guy wanted to put Frankie on another reward program! In their first meeting, Frankie wouldn't even look at Matt. *Can't say that I blame him*, thought Sandra, shaking her head. Matt wouldn't listen to her when she told him about how many stickers and point systems they'd been through. Sandra sighed. *I don't know if I have the energy for this anymore.*

Sandra had always envied the fact that Debbie and Kevin had decent insurance coverage through Kevin's teaching job. Sandra had no such insurance. She had relied exclusively on social service agencies to get Frankie the help he needed.

Sandra took a deep breath. *Enough thinking for one day.* She felt like she was at a crossroads. Her son was slipping away, and the energy and determination that had sustained her through difficult times throughout her life seemed to be fading as well. It was becoming quite clear that energy and determination—and love—weren't going to be enough to make the difference for Frankie.

6

THREE OPTIONS

There are basically three options for handling un-solved problems. I call those options Plan A, Plan B, and Plan C. Plan A refers to solving a problem *unilaterally*. This is where adults decide upon and impose a solution. Plan B involves solving a problem *collaboratively*. And Plan C involves setting aside an unsolved problem, at least for now. If you intend to follow the guidance provided in this book, Plans B and C are your future. Plan A is there if you need it, but you're not going to need it very often, if at all.

By the way, if a child is already reliably meeting a given expectation, you don't need one of the Plans because it's not an unsolved problem. For example, if your child is completing her homework to your satisfaction and without significant difficulty or conflict, you don't need a Plan because your expectation is being met. If your child is brushing her teeth to your satisfaction and without significant difficulty or conflict, you don't need a Plan because the expectation is being met. But if your child is not completing her homework or brushing her teeth in accordance with your expectations, or if these expectations heighten the likelihood of concerning behaviors, you have an unsolved problem and you need a Plan.

Hopefully, by now you've used the ALSUP to identify your child's lagging skills and unsolved problems. Hopefully, you've also decided which high-priority unsolved problems to start working on first (using Plan B) and which you're setting aside for now (Plan C).

Let's take a closer look at the three Plans.

PLAN A

Many people think the terminology *Plan A* refers to the preferred plan. Not so. As you just read, Plan A is where you're solving a problem *unilaterally*, typically through imposition of a solution. With Plan A, *you're* the one deciding on the solution to a given unsolved problem. Your child is a bystander.

The words *"I've decided that . . ."* are usually a good indication that you're in the midst of using Plan A: "Because you're having difficulty completing your math homework before you go outside, *I've decided that* you can't go outside until your math homework is done," or "Because you are having difficulty getting your teeth brushed before bed, *I've decided that* there will be no TV or video games at night until your teeth are brushed," or *"I've decided that* since you seem to be having difficulty being home at 12 am for curfew, you're grounded."

Now, these adult responses to unsolved problems might sound fairly ordinary. That doesn't mean Plan A is the ideal way to solve problems with your child. While you may feel that you are exercising parental authority by using Plan A, you are also inducing frustration. And your child doesn't handle frustration very well. Frustration sets in motion your child's concerning behaviors. And that's not ideal at all. The paradox is that the kids least capable of handling Plan A are the ones most likely to get it, and lots of it. And if a kid is getting lots of Plan A, then Plan A isn't working.

Solutions arrived at through Plan A are not only *unilateral*, but they're also *uninformed*. With Plan A, you're not trying to find out what's making it hard for your child to meet a particular expectation, and you're not trying to address those factors. Uninformed solutions are shots in the dark. Better to take aim.

With Plan A, you're trying to solve the problem through the use of power. Power causes conflict. If you teach power, you'll get power back. In other words, being unilateral is a good way to get your kid to respond in kind.

So, is Plan A off the table completely? No, if your child is about to dart in front of a speeding car in a parking lot, use Plan A. Yank on her arm and save her life. If she blows up, so be it. But, if three weeks later she's darted in front of a speeding car in a parking lot seventeen additional times and you've yanked seventeen additional times, perhaps yanking is effective at saving her life but it's very ineffective at solving the problem. You're going to need a different plan.

The problem is not that caregivers sometimes use Plan A. The problem is that caregivers use Plan A a lot and stick with it even when it's not working.

Does staying away from Plan A mean you're dropping all the expectations you have for your child? No, it doesn't mean that at all. You still have lots of expectations (hopefully they're realistic). What it does mean is that you're going to need another way to solve problems to take the place of Plan A. That's Plan B.

PLAN B

Plan B involves solving a problem *collaboratively*, a process in which you and your child work together to solve the problems that have been setting the stage for challenging episodes and that have been so destructive to your relationship with each other.

According to the conventional wisdom (and many popular parenting books) you should never collaborate with a child. After all, you're in charge. But in this book, being "in charge" means that you understand why, in the case of your child, even the most mundane of problems can set the stage for concerning behaviors, and that you're willing to take action to change course. Don't worry, you're still in charge when you're using Plan B, probably more in charge than you've ever been. The only downside to Plan B is that, at least initially, it's hard to do, primarily because many people haven't had much practice with it.

Plan B consists of three steps, each containing ingredients that are crucial to the collaborative resolution of problems: the Empathy step, the Define Adult Concerns step, and the Invitation step.

1. The *Empathy step* involves gathering information from your child to understand what's making it hard for her to meet a particular expectation.

2. The *Define Adult Concerns step* involves communicating your concern or perspective on the same problem, especially why it's important that the expectation be met.

3. The *Invitation step* is when you and your child work toward a solution that is (a) *realistic* (meaning both parties can actually do what they're agreeing to do) and (b) *mutually satis-*

factory (meaning the solution addresses the concerns of both parties).

On first hearing about Plan B, many caregivers come to the erroneous conclusion that the best time to use Plan B is just as they are in the midst of dealing with an unsolved problem. That's Emergency Plan B, and it's actually not the best timing because the child is already heated up. Few of us do our clearest thinking when we're heated up. As discussed earlier, unsolved problems are highly predictable, so there's no reason to wait until the child gets heated before trying to solve them. The goal is to get the problem solved *ahead of time*, before it comes up again. That's Proactive Plan B. (Of course, if you haven't yet completed the ALSUP for your child—and identified your high-priority unsolved problems—then it will be much more difficult to do Plan B proactively.)

For example, in the case of the unsolved problem of difficulty brushing teeth, the best time to have a Plan B discussion with your child is *before* she's faced with the task of brushing her teeth, rather than in the heat of the moment. If the unsolved problem is difficulty completing math homework, the time to have a Plan B discussion is *before* the next time your child is struggling with her math homework. Since you've already decided which high-priority unsolved problems you're working on, you should be using Proactive Plan B the vast majority of the time.

PLAN C

As you now know, Plan C involves setting aside an unsolved problem completely, at least temporarily. As you've read, Plan C is neither giving in nor giving up. It's prioritizing. If you try solving all of your child's unsolved problems at once, you'll solve none of them at all. When you use Plan C, you've consciously, intentionally, and deliberately decided to set aside a given expectation either because you have other, higher-priority expectations to pursue or because you've decided it was unrealistic in the first place. The biggest downside to Plan C is that some of your expectations won't be met, at least not yet. But the upside is that any unsolved problems you've set aside won't cause concerning behaviors, which means that you and your kid will be more "available" for those unsolved problems that remain and the amount of conflict between you and your child will be reduced.

Many parents feel a little queasy about setting some expectations aside, even for now. Let me help you feel better about it: *she's not currently meeting those expectations anyway.* So, realistically, you have a few options: (1) you could trying working on all of your child's unsolved problems at once (thereby solving none of them and causing both you and your child to become overwhelmed); (2) you could continue to insist that your child meet expectations you already know she can't reliably meet (causing countless unnecessary concerning behaviors but coming no closer to having the expectations be met); or (3) you could make it official: you don't expect your child to meet those expectations right now. Option number three is Plan C. You aren't shirking parental responsibility by prioritizing.

As with Plan B, the form of Plan C you want to be using most often is Proactive Plan C. If you've decided that brushing teeth is a low-priority unsolved problem, you wouldn't tell your child to brush her teeth. If you've decided that homework completion is a low-priority unsolved problem for now, then you wouldn't tell your child to do her homework. When will you start mentioning these things again? After you've solved some higher-priority unsolved problems and can turn your attention to some of the ones you've set aside.

Proactive Plan C can also involve coming up with an interim plan for an unsolved problem that has been set aside for now. Here's what that might sound like:

DEBBIE: Jennifer, you know how Dad and I are always getting on your case about eating dinner together as a family?
JENNIFER: I don't want to talk about that!
DEBBIE: Oh, I don't want to talk about it either. I just wanted to let you know that we're not going to bug you about it anymore. You don't have to eat dinner with us if you don't want to.
JENNIFER: I don't?
DEBBIE: No, there are some other problems that are

more important for us to work on, so we're just going to let that one go for now.

JENNIFER: So, I can eat wherever I want?

DEBBIE: Well, that's what I wanted to talk to you about for a second. I was thinking we could come up with a plan for places it's OK to eat dinner and places it's not. There are two places I'd really prefer that you not eat.

JENNIFER: Where?

DEBBIE: Your bedroom and the living room.

JENNIFER: Can I eat in the TV room?

DEBBIE: Yes, that's fine with me . . . just not your bedroom and the living room. Are you good with that?

JENNIFER: Yep. So, I don't have to eat dinner with you guys if I don't want to?

DEBBIE: That's right . . . for now anyway.

JENNIFER: What if I want to eat dinner with you?

DEBBIE: You're welcome to eat dinner with us if you want to . . . but you don't have to. Good?

JENNIFER: Yep.

What if you slip and direct your child to do something that you've already identified as a low-priority unsolved problem? Use Emergency Plan C and simply say "OK."

PARENT: Thomas, it's time for you to brush your teeth.

THOMAS: I'm not brushing my teeth.

PARENT: OK.

In the next chapter, we're going to sink our teeth into the three ingredients of Plan B. But first let's answer a few questions.

Q & A

QUESTION: Let me get this straight: I'm supposed to drop all my expectations so my kid doesn't get upset anymore?
ANSWER: You can't raise a child or run a household without expectations. So, no, you're definitely not dropping all of your expectations. But you are prioritizing, because you can't solve everything at once. The unsolved problems you're setting aside for now (Plan C) will make it easier for you to work on your high-priority unsolved problems with Plan B.

QUESTION: Isn't this just about picking battles?
ANSWER: No, it's definitely not about picking battles. The fact that your child is having difficulty meeting an expectation doesn't mean there's a battle; it means there's a problem to solve. Battle picking is the unenviable scenario of feeling that you only have two options: pursue an expectation through the imposition of adult will (knowing full well that doing so will cause a battle) or avoid the battle (but at the price of not pursuing important expectations).

QUESTION: So, I'm not allowed to tell my kid what to do anymore?

ANSWER: It depends on what you mean by *telling*. If *telling* means you're simply reminding your child of an expectation—for example, "Kids, it's time to go brush your teeth"—then you may not be out of the telling business. But if you find yourself "telling" your child to do the same thing over and over again, then telling isn't working and you'll need to use Plan B to find out why your child is having difficulty meeting the expectation you keep telling her about. Of course, if what you mean by "telling" is that you're deciding what the solution is to a given unsolved problem, that's Plan A.

QUESTION: I can't set limits anymore?
ANSWER: Plan A isn't the only way to set limits. You're setting limits when you're using Plan B, too. You're probably reading this book right now because the Plan A way of setting limits hasn't panned out so well for you and your child.

QUESTION: So, the problems I really care about, that's Plan A. And the problems I sort of care about, that's Plan B. And the problems I don't care about at all, that's Plan C. Right?
ANSWER: Not right. The Plans are not a ranking system. Each Plan represents a distinct way of responding to unsolved problems.

7

PLAN B

In this chapter we get into the nitty-gritty of each of the three steps of Plan B. You'll find additional nitty-gritty in chapter 8, especially related to difficulties you may encounter in your efforts to use Plan B.

THE EMPATHY STEP

The goal of the Empathy step is to *gather information from your child to understand what's making it difficult for them to meet a certain expectation*. If you don't gather that information, the problem will remain unsolved. Just like the rest of us, kids have legitimate concerns: hunger, fatigue, fear, the desire to buy or do certain things, the tendency to avoid things that are scary or that make them uncomfortable or at which they don't feel competent.

Some adults have never thought it was especially important to gather information about and understand what's making it hard for a kid to meet an expectation. That's why many kids are accustomed to having their concerns dismissed or disregarded by adults who have concerns of their own or who feel that they already know what's getting in the kid's way on a given problem. Kids who are accustomed to having their concerns dismissed tend to be far less receptive to hearing the concerns of their caregivers. Over time, such kids also become far less receptive to talking to their parents. The number one complaint I get from kids is that their parents don't listen; and the number one complaint I get from parents is that their kids won't talk to them.

The Empathy step gives your child a voice. Then they don't have to scream—or exhibit any other concerning behaviors—to be heard. And, just in case you had any doubts, it's good for children to be heard.

When you enter the Empathy step you do so with *curiosity* and the recognition that you don't yet know what's making it hard for your child to meet a particular expectation. As you've read, it's very common for parents to find that what they *thought* was making it hard for their child to meet an expectation is *not* what was making it hard for the child to meet an expectation. So, the pressure's off: there's no need to divine your child's concern or perspective. You don't need to be a mind reader. But you do need to become highly skilled at gathering information from your child.

The Empathy step begins with an introduction to the unsolved problem. The introduction usually begins with the words *"I've noticed that . . ."* and ends with the words *"What's up?"* In between you're inserting the unsolved problem. The introduction is made much easier if you stick with the guidelines for writing unsolved problems you read about in chapter 4. Remember, if you don't stick with the guidelines, you reduce the likelihood of the kid participating in the process. If they don't participate, you won't understand what's making it hard for them to meet the expectation, the problem will remain unsolved, and the concerning behaviors that are being caused by the problem will persist. Here are some examples:

"I've noticed that it's been difficult for you to go to school lately. What's up?"

"I've noticed that it's been difficult for you to brush your teeth before going to bed at night. What's up?"

"I've noticed that it's been difficult for you to complete your math homework lately. What's up?"

"I've noticed that it's been difficult for you to stick with the thirty-minute time limit on playing video games. What's up?"

"I've noticed that it's been hard for you to get to bed by 9 pm lately. What's up?"

"I've noticed that it's been difficult for you to get to the school bus by 7:45 am lately. What's up?"

After you ask, "What's up?" one of five things is going to happen next:

- **POSSIBILITY #1:** The child says something.

- **POSSIBILITY #2:** The child says nothing or "I don't know."

- **POSSIBILITY #3:** The child says, "I don't have a problem with that" or "I don't care."

- **POSSIBILITY #4:** The child says, "I don't want to talk about it right now."

- **POSSIBILITY #5:** The child becomes defensive and says something like "I don't have to talk to you" (or worse).

Let's make sure you're prepared for each of these possibilities.

The Child Says Something

If the introduction to an unsolved problem elicits a response from the child, that's good. However, the child's initial response seldom provides a clear understanding of their concern or perspective, so you're going to need to probe for more information. I call this probing process "drilling," and there's no doubt that drilling is the hardest part of all of Plan B. It's where most Plan B ships run aground (and where most captains abandon ship). The good news is that there are some strategies to help you master the drilling process so the Plan B boat stays afloat.

First, notice the word is *drill*, not *grill*. The primary goal of drilling is to *clarify*, whereas grilling tends to be an act of intimidation. Your goal is to demonstrate to your child that your attempt to understand their concern or perspective isn't fake or perfunctory—*you really want to understand*.

Second, *drilling* is not the same thing as *talking*. There are caregivers who frequently talk to (or at) a kid, but never achieve a clear understanding of what's making it hard for the kid to meet an expectation.

Drilling is hard because a lot of caregivers haven't had much practice at gathering information from kids. They aren't sure how to go about doing it. Here are the drilling strategies, followed by examples:

Strategy #1: *Reflective listening*—simply saying back to the child whatever they just said to you—often followed by clarifying statements, like "How so?" or "I don't quite understand" or "I'm confused" or "Can you say more about that?" or "What do you mean?" This is your default drilling strategy, and the one you'll be using most often. If you're drilling and you get stuck and aren't sure what to say, reflective listening and clarifying statements are always a safe bet.

Strategy #2: Asking questions beginning with the words *who, what, where,* or *when.*

Strategy #3: Asking about the *situational variability* of the unsolved problem; in other words, why is the child meeting the expectation sometimes and not other times?

Strategy #4: Asking the child what they're *thinking* in the midst of the unsolved problem. Notice it doesn't say *feeling.* While it's fine to understand a child's feelings in response to an unsolved problem, asking about what they're *thinking* is more likely to provide information about what's making it hard to meet the expectation.

Strategy #5: Breaking the unsolved problem down into its *component parts.* Many unsolved problems—for example, getting ready for bed at night, getting ready for school in the morning—have multiple components. But kids sometimes need help identifying those components so they can pinpoint which component is causing them difficulty.

Strategy #6: Making a *discrepant observation.* This is where you're making an observation that differs from information that the child has already provided in the Empathy step. It's the riskiest of the drilling strategies, because some kids are going to interpret a discrepant observation as an indication that you think they're lying. You don't think they're lying— kids are entitled to their beliefs about the factors that are making it hard to meet an expectation—you just have observations that differ.

Strategy #7: *Summarizing and asking for more.* This is where you're recapping what the child has already told you in the Empathy step and asking if there are any other factors that are making it hard for them to meet the expectation. It's a good organizational strategy; it helps keep track of the concerns the child has already expressed. It also helps you know when the Empathy step is done. If the child can't think of any other factors that are making it hard to meet an expectation, the Empathy step is done and you're ready to move on to the next step.

Strategy #8: *Tabling and asking for more.* This strategy is very similar to summarizing, except that instead of recapping what the child has told you, you're metaphorically sidelining those concerns so the child can think of any other factors that are making it hard for them to meet the expectation.

Here's an example of what drilling might sound like, with the number of each specific drilling strategy in parentheses:

PARENT: I've noticed that you've been having difficulty getting started on the Shakespeare paper for homework. What's up?"

ANA: It's too hard.

PARENT (Strategies #1 and #2): It's too hard . . . what part is too hard?

ANA: It's too much.

PARENT (Strategies #1 and #2 again): It's too much. I don't understand . . . what's too much?

ANA: The writing part is too much.

PARENT (Strategies #1 and #2): Ah, the writing part is too much. When is the writing part too much?

ANA: I don't know.

PARENT: Take your time. We're not in a rush.

ANA: I've never written a paper this long before. I don't know what to say. And I don't know what words to use to get started.

PARENT (Strategy #7): Ah, so you've never written a paper this long before, and you don't know what to say, and you don't know what words to use to get started.

ANA: Yes! It's too hard!

PARENT (Strategy #2): Well, I'm glad we're figuring this out. But I'm still a little confused. What is it about the length of the paper that's hard for you?

ANA: There's different sections, and I'm supposed to write about each of them.

PARENT (Strategy #1): There's different sections and you're supposed to write about each of them. Tell me more.

ANA: I don't know how to start each section.

PARENT (Strategies #1 and #2): You don't know how to start each section. What's hard about that?

ANA: I can't think of the words! I already said that!

PARENT (Strategies #1 and #2): Yes, you did say that. I'm just trying to understand what's hard about that.

ANA: I mostly know what I want to write. I just can't think of the words to start writing it.

PARENT (Strategy #1): So, you know what you want to say . . . but thinking of the words to start saying it is the hard part.

ANA: Yes.

PARENT (Strategy #8): So, if you weren't having difficulty thinking of the words to start writing each section, is there anything else that would make it hard for you to get started on the Shakespeare paper?

ANA: No. I don't think so. Could you just write it for me?

PARENT: I suppose I could do that. We'll think of solutions in a few minutes. But I'm very glad I understand what's been hard for you.

Very informative. We went all the way from "It's too hard" to "I can't think of the words to start saying what I want to say" and came away with a much clearer sense of what's making it hard for Ana to meet the expectation.

Adults are often astonished by what they learn when they start inquiring about a kid's concerns. Let's see what information turns up with the other examples we discussed previously (all of which would then require further drilling):

ADULT: I've noticed that it's been difficult for you to get to school lately. What's up?

KID: Sophie's been hitting me on the playground.

ADULT: I've noticed that it's been difficult for you to brush your teeth at night. What's up?
KID: I don't like the taste of the toothpaste.

ADULT: I've noticed that it's been difficult for you to stick with the 30-minute time limit on playing video games. What's up?
KID: I don't have anyone to play with. No one in the neighborhood wants to play with me.

ADULT: I've noticed that it's been hard for you to get to bed on time lately. What's up?
KID: I don't like being alone in the dark.

ADULT: I've noticed that it's been hard for you to wake up in the morning to get to school lately. What's up?
KID: Ever since we started that new medicine, I'm really tired in the morning.

ADULT: I've noticed that it's been difficult for you to get to the school bus on time in the morning. What's up?
KID: I don't want to take the school bus anymore. The bus driver always blames me when there's trouble.

Some adults, having now made some headway toward understanding their kids' concerns, have difficulty resisting the temptation to revert to form by being dismissive or offering solutions, thereby ending the problem-solving process. Here are some examples of what *not* to do:

> **ADULT:** I've noticed that it's been difficult for you to get to school lately. What's up?
>
> **KID:** Sophie's been hitting me on the playground.
>
> **ADULT:** Well, you should just hit her back.

> **ADULT:** I've noticed that it's been difficult for you to brush your teeth at night. What's up?
>
> **KID:** I don't like the taste of the toothpaste.
>
> **ADULT:** I don't like the taste of the toothpaste either, but that doesn't stop me from brushing my teeth.

> **ADULT:** I've noticed that it's been difficult for you to stick with the 30-minute time limit on playing video games. What's up?
>
> **KID:** I don't have anyone to play with. No one in the neighborhood wants to play with me.
>
> **ADULT:** Oh, you have lots of friends. I think you're just making excuses.

> **ADULT:** I've noticed that it's been hard for you to get to bed on time lately. What's up?
>
> **KID:** I don't like being alone in the dark.
>
> **ADULT:** Oh, you'll be fine.

ADULT: I've noticed that it's been hard for you to wake up in the morning to get to school lately. What's up?

KID: Ever since we started that new medicine, I'm really tired in the morning.

ADULT: I think you just need to try harder.

ADULT: I've noticed that it's been difficult for you to get to the school bus on time in the morning. What's up?

KID: I don't want to take the school bus anymore. The bus driver always blames me when there's trouble.

ADULT: So just stay away from the kids who cause trouble, and the bus driver won't blame you.

The Child Says Nothing or "I Don't Know"

While it would be great if kids always said something in response to "What's up?" and if they knew exactly how to explain themselves, that's often not the case. In fact, it's pretty common for kids to say nothing or "I don't know" over the course of the Empathy step. If a kid says nothing or "I don't know" right off the bat, you'll want to do some self-assessment: Are you using Plan A instead of Plan B? Are you using Emergency Plan B rather than Proactive Plan B? Did you word your unsolved problem according to the guidelines?

Some kids say nothing or "I don't know" in the Empathy step because they're collecting their thoughts, in which case you'd simply want to respond with patience and encouragement, perhaps by saying, "I guess I've never asked you about this before. Take your time. We're not in a rush." Unfortunately, we adults often feel pressure to fill the void with our own theories (e.g., "I think the reason you're spending so much time playing video games is because you don't want to do your chores"). In such instances, you've strayed quite a bit from the main goal of the Empathy step (information-gathering) and made it even more difficult for your kid to think. You may need to grow more comfortable with the silence that can occur as a kid is giving thought to their concerns.

One of the advantages of doing Plan B in a planned, proactive manner is that you're not surprising the child with the timing or topic of the discussion. Indeed, it often makes good sense to make an appointment with your child. It's also a good idea to give the child advance notice of what it is that you're going to be talking about.

The Child Says, "I Don't Have a Problem with That" or "I Don't Care"

This response can cause great panic in adults, especially if they're wondering whether it's possible to solve a problem if the kid doesn't think the problem is actually a problem. The child may indeed be saying that they aren't as concerned about the problem as their caregivers might be (they may not care if their bedroom is messy, may not find it compelling to get to bed on time, and may not feel great urgency about coming home in time for curfew). But that's not a showstopper;

it's actually the beginning of learning more about the kid's concern or perspective. The first drilling strategy (reflective listening) should serve you well in such instances: "Ah, so you don't feel that coming home in time for curfew is a major concern. I don't quite understand. Can you tell me more about that?" Another possibility is that the child is really saying something else (and the same strategy would help clarify what they really mean). Here's an example:

PARENT: I've noticed that you've been having difficulty keeping your room clean. What's up?

KID: I don't have a problem with that.

PARENT: Ah, you don't have a problem with that. You're good with your room being messy?

KID: I didn't say that.

PARENT: I'm sorry, I thought I heard you say you didn't have a problem with your room being messy.

KID: Well, I don't have as big a problem with it as you do.

PARENT: Oh, I missed that. So, you don't have as big a problem with it as I do. Do you mind your room being messy?

KID: Yeah.

PARENT: What's getting in the way of your room being cleaner?

KID: Well, at this point it's so messy, I wouldn't know where to start on cleaning it. I think I'm going to need some help.

The Child Says, "I Don't Want to Talk About It Right Now"

This response can throw adults off their game as well. The reality is that the child doesn't have to talk about it right now, and it's good to let them know that. Lots of kids start talking the instant they're given permission *not* to talk. Second, if they truly don't want to talk about it right now, maybe they'll talk about why. A lot of kids will talk about *why* they don't want to talk about something, which is very informative in its own right. Then, after they're through talking about that, they're comfortable enough to start talking about what they didn't want to talk about in the first place. Here's the take-home message: Don't try so hard to get your kid to talk today that you decrease the likelihood that they'll talk to you tomorrow. There's always tomorrow.

The Child Becomes Defensive and Says Something Like "I Don't Have to Talk to You"

First, it's important to consider why a child would become defensive in response to adult requests for information on a particular unsolved problem, and there are lots of potential reasons. Maybe they're accustomed to problems being solved unilaterally (Plan A), or think that if a problem is being raised they must be in trouble, so they're anticipating the lowering of the boom. Maybe they don't really see the point in contemplating or voicing their concerns since they're accustomed to having them dismissed or disregarded.

The best response to defensive statements is not reciprocal defensiveness but rather honesty. A good response to "I don't have to talk to you" would be "You don't have to talk to me." A good response to "You're not my boss" would be "I'm not your boss." And a good response to "You can't make me talk" would be "I can't make you talk." Some reassurance that you're not using Plan A might be helpful, as in "I'm not telling you what to do" (you're not), "You're not in trouble" (they're not), "I'm not mad at you" (you're not), and "I'm just trying to understand" (you are). Notice I'm excluding statements like "I just want what's best for you" and "I'm doing this (Plan A) because I love you."

Are you wondering if your child has sufficient language processing and verbal communication skills to participate in Plan B? There's no question that the dialogues you've already read show what Plan B looks like with kids who have these skills. In chapter 9 you'll read about how to adjust things for kids who are having difficulty participating in Plan B because of the lack of these skills (or other reasons).

THE DEFINE ADULT CONCERNS STEP

The primary goal of the Define Adult Concerns step is to enter your concern or perspective into consideration. This step usually begins with the words "*My concern is . . ."* or *"The thing is . . ."* (you'll see many examples in the coming pages).

This step is made difficult primarily by the fact that adults frequently haven't given much thought to their concerns about unsolved problems, often because they've been more focused on their *solutions* to those problems. But you shouldn't be thinking about solutions in the Define Adult Concerns step. *There's really no point in thinking of solutions until the concerns of both parties have been identified.*

Adult concerns are related to *why it's important that an expectation be met,* and typically involve one or both of two categories:

- *How the problem is affecting the kid* (health, safety, learning)

- *How the problem is affecting others* (health, safety, learning)

Let's see what some adult concerns might be on some of the problems we considered previously:

- **DIFFICULTY GOING TO SCHOOL:** The thing is, if you don't go to school, I'm concerned that you're going to miss out on a lot of important learning.

- **DIFFICULTY BRUSHING TEETH AT NIGHT:** The thing is, if you don't brush your teeth at night, the food you've been eating all day sits on your teeth and could cause cavities. I'm not all that interested in spending money for the dentist, and I don't want you to have to go through the agony of getting Novocaine and having your teeth drilled.

- **DIFFICULTY COMPLETING MATH HOMEWORK:** My concern is that you're missing out on a lot of important practice by not doing your homework. Plus, if you just skip the math homework, we won't know the parts of math that are hard for you.

- **DIFFICULTY STICKING WITH THE 30-MINUTE LIMIT ON VIDEO GAMES:** My concern is that all that time alone in front of video games isn't making it any more likely that the other kids in the neighborhood will want to play with you. And it's making it harder for you to get around to your chores.

- **DIFFICULTY GETTING TO BED ON TIME:** The thing is, when you get to bed late, you're tired at school the next day and you have trouble concentrating and getting your work done in your classes.

- **DIFFICULTY WAKING UP IN THE MORNING:** My concern is that when you have difficulty waking up in the morning, you end up being late for school, and you're falling behind in your first two classes because you're frequently not there in time to attend.

- **DIFFICULTY GETTING TO THE SCHOOL BUS ON TIME:** My concern is that, when you miss the school bus, I have to take you to school myself, and my boss is getting a little upset about me coming in late.

Earlier in this chapter you read an Empathy step that was done with Ana on the problem of difficulty completing the Shakespeare paper for homework. No reason to have you read the entire Empathy step again here. But here's what the Define Adult Concerns step would have sounded like on that one:

PARENT: The thing is, if you don't write the Shakespeare paper, then you won't get any practice at starting the paragraphs and it will always be hard for you. Plus, it would be a shame for that to get in the way of you getting your paper done, since you know what you want to write and you have really good ideas.

Two sets of concerns are on the table. No turning back now.

THE INVITATION STEP

In this final step you and your child are working together to come up with a solution. It's called the Invitation step because the adult actually invites the child to solve the problem collaboratively. The Invitation step lets the child know that solving the problem is something you're doing with them (collaboratively) rather than to them (unilaterally).

To start this step, you could simply say something like "Let's think about how we can solve this problem" or "Let's think about how we can work that out." But to be as explicit as possible, I recommend that you recap the two concerns that were identified in the first two steps, usually starting with the words *"I wonder if there's a way."* So, in the previous example, that would sound something like this: *"I wonder if there's a way for us to help you find the words to start each section . . ."* (that was the kid's concern) *". . . and still make sure you get some practice at doing that so it won't always be so hard for you and so that you can express your really good ideas"* (that was the adult's concern).

Then you give the kid the first crack at generating a solution: *"Do you have any ideas?"* This is not an indication that the burden for solving the problem is placed solely on the kid. The burden for solving the problem is placed on the problem-solving partners: your child and you. But giving kids the first crack at thinking of a solution is a good strategy; it lets them know you're actually interested in their ideas.

Many parents, in their eagerness to solve the problem, forget the Invitation step. This means that just as they are at the precipice of actually collaborating on a solution, they impose a solution. Too often we assume that the only person capable of coming up with a good solution to a problem is the adult. While there is some chance that your kid won't be able to think of any solutions—an issue discussed in greater detail in chapter 8—there's actually an outstanding chance your child can think of good solutions. There's also a good chance they have been waiting (not so patiently) for the chance to do that.

When you use Plan B, you do so with the understanding that the solution is not predetermined. If you already know how the problem is going to be solved before you start trying to solve it, then you're not using Plan B . . . you're using a "clever" form of Plan A. Plan B is not just a "clever" form of Plan A. Plan B is collaborative, Plan A is unilateral.

When it comes to Plan B, you're off the hook for coming up with an instantaneous, ingenious solution to the problems your child encounters. You'd think that would be a relief for many parents, but the reality is that it takes some getting used to. The truth is that your unilateral solutions weren't working very well anyway. Though it may have felt like coming up with a quick, unilateral solution to a problem was a time-saver, solutions that aren't working take an enormous amount of time, including the amount of time you spend dealing with the concerning behaviors that are a by-product of those solutions.

This next part is crucial (you read a little about it in the previous chapter). There are two criteria for gauging whether a solution is going to get the job done, and these criteria should be considered and discussed by you and your child before signing on the dotted line: the solution must be *realistic* (meaning both parties can actually do what they're agreeing to do) and *mutually satisfactory* (meaning the solution truly and logically addresses the concerns of both parties). If a solution isn't realistic and mutually satisfactory, the problem isn't solved yet and the problem-solving partners are still working on it.

The realistic part is important because Plan B isn't an exercise in wishful thinking. If you can't execute your part of the solution that's under consideration, don't agree to it just to end the conversation. Likewise, if you don't think your kid can execute their part of the solution that's under consideration, then try to get them to take a moment to think about whether they can actually do what they're agreeing to do (*"You sure you can do that? Let's make sure we come up with a solution we can both do"*). By the way, "trying harder" is never a viable solution.

The mutually satisfactory part is important, too, and is of great comfort to adults who fear that in using Plan B their concerns will go unaddressed and no limits will be set. You're "setting limits" if your concerns are being addressed. If a solution is mutually satisfactory, then by definition your concerns have been addressed. So, if you thought that Plan A is the only mechanism by which adults can set limits, you were mistaken. And if your concerns are being addressed with Plan B, then why do you still need Plan A? Maybe you don't.

The mutually satisfactory part also helps the kid know that *you're as invested in ensuring that their concerns are addressed as you are in making sure that yours are addressed.* That's how you lose an enemy and gain a problem-solving partner. That's how you move from adversary to teammate.

Early on, many kids have a tendency to think of solutions that will address *their* concerns but not *yours* (many adults have the same tendency). In such instances, simply remind the child that the goal is to come up with a solution that works for both of you, perhaps by saying, *"Well, that's an idea, and I know that idea would address your concern, but I don't think it would address my concern. Let's see if we can come up with an idea that will work for both of us."* In other words, there's no such thing as a bad solution—only solutions that aren't realistic or mutually satisfactory.

Let's see how the Invitation step might have progressed with Ana:

PARENT: I wonder if there's a way for us to help you find the words to start each section and still make sure you get some practice at doing that so it won't always be so hard for you and so that you can express your really good ideas. Do you have any ideas?

ANA: Um . . . no.

PARENT: Well, take your time. We've never really talked about it like this before. If you don't have any ideas, maybe I can come up with some.

ANA: It's so stupid that I can't come up with the words.

PARENT: I know it's very frustrating for you. But maybe that's because it isn't solved yet. I bet there's a way for us to solve this.

ANA: It's not like the beginning of every section has to be super-original.

PARENT: No, probably not. There probably aren't that many ways to begin each section.

ANA: Could we come up with a few beginnings? Like, write down, like, four or five ways for me to start a paragraph?

PARENT: We could try that. Do you think that would help?

ANA: We can find out.

PARENT: Let's do it. I wonder if we should also ask your teacher, Mrs. Abernathy, if she has any ideas.

ANA: Let's see if our idea works first. If it doesn't work, we can ask her.

PARENT: OK. Let's think about whether our solution is realistic. I think we can both do what we're agreeing to do. Yes?

ANA: Yes.

PARENT: Would it address your concern? That you're having difficulty finding the words to start each section?

ANA: If it works it would.

PARENT: And it would address my concern that the paper isn't getting done and that you aren't expressing your great ideas. Shall we give it a shot?

ANA: OK.

PARENT: And if that solution doesn't work, we'll talk some more and come up with one that does.
ANA: OK.

The parent's last line was significant, as it underscores a very important point: it's good for the kid and adult to acknowledge that the problem may require additional discussion, because there's actually a decent chance that *the first solution won't solve the problem durably.*

Why wouldn't the first solution solve the problem durably? Often because the solution wasn't as realistic or mutually satisfactory as it first seemed. Good reasons to go back to Plan B to come up with a solution that is more realistic and truly mutually satisfactory. It's also possible that the first attempt at clarifying concerns yielded useful but incomplete information. By definition, the solution will only address the concerns you identified, but can't possibly address the ones you haven't identified.

In real life, solving a problem that has been causing major disagreements for a long time often isn't a one-shot deal. Good solutions—durable ones—are usually refined versions of the solutions that came before them.

It's also important to mention that Plan B isn't usually this easy, especially early on. For example, sometimes kids (and even adults) get pretty heated up while using Plan B. Sometimes this is because history has taught them that disagreements are always handled using Plan A. It may take a while (and a lot of Plan B) for the child's instantaneous heated reaction to unsolved problems to subside. Adults sometimes become impatient in the midst of Plan B and head for Plan A or Plan C. Hang in there.

Are you wondering about the difference between Emergency Plan B and Proactive Plan B? They differ on two counts: the timing and the wording of the Empathy step. Because Emergency Plan B typically occurs in hurried conditions and after a kid is already heated up, it isn't ideal for gathering information and solving problems durably. So, while Emergency Plan B is available to you as an option, you don't want to make a habit of it. The Define Adult Concerns step and the Invitation step are much the same with Emergency Plan B as with Proactive Plan B (though they're often louder and more intense under emergent conditions). The Empathy step of Emergency Plan B wouldn't begin with an introduction (as in Proactive Plan B) because it's already too late. So, you'd head straight into reflective listening. Here are a few examples of what that would sound like:

KID: I'm not taking my meds.
ADULT: You're not taking your meds. What's up?

KID: I'm not going to school today.
ADULT: You're not going to school today. What's up?

KID: This homework sucks!
ADULT: You're frustrated about your homework. What's up?

Now, a caveat: while as a general rule Proactive Plan B is far preferable to Emergency Plan B, there are some kids—they are few and far between, but they exist—who have difficulty participating in Proactive Plan B because they have trouble remembering the specifics of problems you're trying to discuss. For these kids, the problem is only memorable and salient when they're in the midst of it. Early on, Emergency Plan B may actually be preferable for these kids. I've found that many of these kids are able to participate in proactive discussions once Plan B becomes more familiar to them.

• • •

Are you ready to try your first Plan B with your child? Maybe not, but no time like the present. Pick one of your high-priority unsolved problems, make an appointment with your kid, and try using Proactive Plan B to solve it. If it goes well, fantastic. If it doesn't go well—and, this being a new skill, there's a decent chance it won't—keep reading.

• • •

Here's a brief summary of what you've just read:

- Plan B consists of three steps or ingredients:
  - The Empathy Step: Gathering information about and understanding what's making it

hard for your child to meet a given expectation.

- The Define Adult Concerns Step: Being specific about why it's important that the expectation be met (how the problem is affecting the kid and/or others).
- The Invitation Step: Collaborating with your child to find a solution that is realistic and mutually satisfactory.

- There are two forms of Plan B, depending on timing: Emergency Plan B and Proactive Plan B. Because Proactive Plan B is far preferable, it's been the primary focus of this chapter. Emergency Plan B—because of added heat and time pressure—is much harder and much less likely to lead to durable solutions.

- Like any new skill, Plan B can be challenging, and it takes time to get good at it. The more you practice, the easier Plan B becomes. Plan B isn't something you do two or three times before returning to your old way of doing things. It's not a technique; it's a way of life.

• • •

Debbie and Kevin had agreed that it might be a little less overwhelming for everyone if Debbie tried doing the first Plan B with Jennifer on her own. A few days earlier, Debbie had told Jennifer that there was something she wanted to understand better about a problem they were having and asked if they could talk over the weekend. Debbie thought Jennifer would balk at the idea, so she was surprised when Jennifer agreed. Debbie knew it would be best to give Jennifer advance notice of what she wanted to talk about, but Jennifer didn't seem interested in knowing what Debbie wanted to talk about, and Debbie feared that Jennifer would refuse to talk if she was explicit about the topic. They agreed to talk during breakfast on Saturday morning. Kevin and Riley were already at hockey practice.

"Jennifer, remember there was something I said I wanted to understand better and we agreed to talk about it during breakfast this morning?" Debbie began, sitting down at the kitchen table with Jennifer.

Jennifer grunted through a mouthful of waffles.

Debbie continued. "I was hoping we could talk about the difficulty you and Riley have when you're watching TV together."

"He should just let me watch what I want. I'm the older sister," said Jennifer.

Debbie knew Jennifer had just proposed a solution and knew they weren't supposed to be talking about solutions yet. "That's an interesting idea." Debbie wasn't sure what to say next. Then she remembered that her default strategy was reflective listening. "So, you're the older sister and you feel you should be able to watch what you want."

"Uh-huh."

Debbie was briefly at a loss. She was pretty surprised that Jennifer was participating in the conversation. That was good.

Jennifer wasn't screaming or running out of the room. That was good, too. But what to say next? Debbie opted for a clarifying question. "Can you tell me more about that?"

Jennifer wiped some maple syrup from her lips. "Not really."

This is hard! thought Debbie. She tried thinking about the drilling strategies. She resisted the temptation to jump quickly to the Define Adult Concerns step. Though it felt interminable to Debbie, Jennifer didn't seem to mind the silence. Debbie went with a different drilling strategy. "You know, I'm not even sure I know what it is that you guys are disagreeing about when you're watching TV. Can you tell me about that?"

"Riley always wants to watch *SportsCenter*, and I hate *SportsCenter*. All he thinks about is sports."

More info! thought Debbie. She stuck with reflective listening. "So, Riley always wants to watch *SportsCenter*." Then she went with the second drilling strategy. "What do you want to watch?"

"Anything besides *SportsCenter*," said Jennifer. "I like *Dance Moms*. Or *Say Yes to the Dress*. He hates those shows." Jennifer paused. "Why are we talking about this anyway? He should just let me watch what I want. I'm the older sister."

Debbie was briefly stumped by Jennifer's return to her previous stance but was finding that she was actually curious about her daughter's view on this issue. "Tell me more about that."

"I'm the older sister."

"Yes, you are the older sister. But help me understand why that means that you should pick what's on the TV."

"Because I was here first."

Debbie was alarmed to see that Jennifer was now getting up from the table. "Where are you going, honey?"

"I'm done with my breakfast," said Jennifer.

"Yes, but we're not done talking," said Debbie.

"I am," said Jennifer. She left the kitchen and went to her room.

Debbie hadn't expected the conversation to end so abruptly, though it had lasted much longer than she'd anticipated. She tried to process what had just happened. On the one hand, she was sorry that the conversation hadn't lasted longer. They didn't even make it all the way through the Empathy step! On the other hand, Jennifer had talked! She provided some information! She didn't blow up! Maybe she'll talk again! "Problem solving is incremental," she whispered to herself, quoting something she'd read on a new website.

8

THE NUANCES

How did your first attempt at Plan B go? If, in the Empathy step, you learned about what's making it hard for your child to meet one of your expectations, that's good. If, in the Define Adult Concerns step, you resisted the temptation to put your solutions on the table and instead were able to pinpoint why it's important that the expectation be met, that's good, too. If you made it to the Invitation step and were able to collaborate with your child on a realistic and mutually satisfactory solution, that's also good. Hopefully, the solution you and your child agreed upon will stand the test of time. If it doesn't, you'll find out soon enough, and then it's back to Plan B to figure out why and to come up with a solution that is more realistic and mutually satisfactory than the first one, or one that addresses concerns that may not have been identified in your first try. When you think the time is right, move on to another unsolved problem.

But if things didn't go so well, don't despair. As you already know, it can take a while for you and your child to become good at this. Plan B can go astray for a variety of reasons. Let's take a closer look at some patterns that may be getting in the way. Several of the points were covered earlier in this chapter. The repetition is intentional—just trying to make sure you didn't miss anything.

YOU HAVEN'T TRIED PLAN B YET

Maybe you don't feel very confident about your incipient Plan B skills, so you're a little reluctant to give it a whirl. That's understandable, given that you've probably had a lot more practice at Plan A. Or perhaps you're worried that your child will respond to Plan B with the same heated and volatile reaction that has always been the case with Plan A. We can't rule out that possibility completely; some kids are so accustomed to Plan A that they don't immediately recognize that you're trying hard to do things a different way. So, you may have some residual heat to contend with. But if you never give Plan B a try, then you and your kid will never become good at it. No one is great at Plan B in the beginning. You and your child are becoming good at this together.

YOU'VE TRIED PLAN B, BUT YOU'RE RELYING PRIMARILY ON EMERGENCY PLAN B INSTEAD OF PROACTIVE PLAN B

Remember, Emergency Plan B involves more heat (as in heat of the moment), more rush (as in you're in the middle of something or on your way somewhere), and less ideal circumstances (for example, you're driving the car, you're in a parking lot or in the middle of a department store and have other kids and people around). All of those factors are likely to work against you when you're trying to solve a problem collaboratively. You have much better odds if you're going about it proactively. That's why the ALSUP is so important: it sets the stage for you to identify unsolved problems and decide on high-priority unsolved problems ahead of time.

If you're not the methodical, organized type, being proactive could be a challenge. Yet, being in perpetual crisis mode is probably even more challenging. Solving problems collaboratively, improving your relationship with your kid, and enhancing the skills he needs to handle problems and frustrations more adaptively is likely to require that you make some adjustments to your standard operating procedure.

If you're extremely busy and are accustomed to solving problems in the spur of the moment, there's a good chance you're leaving your kid floundering in your wake, and he's probably not doing very well back there. We could demand that *he* adapt to *you*, but since flexibility and adaptability are not his strengths, the more realistic option (though it may not be easy) is for *you* to adapt to *him*. Once he learns some skills and you are able to solve some chronic problems together, maybe he'll be able to reciprocate.

YOU'RE USING PLAN B AS A LAST RESORT
Plan B isn't an act of desperation, and it's not something you turn to only when Plan A has failed you.

YOU STILL HAVE YOUR OLD LENSES ON
If you're still not convinced that your kid lacks the skills to be flexible, handle frustration, and solve problems, you may want to go back and reread chapters 2 and 3. Don't forget, the alternative explanation—that your child is attention-seeking, manipulative, coercive, limit-testing, and unmotivated, and that you're a passive, permissive, inconsistent, non-contingent disciplinarian—hasn't made things any better, so you really don't have a lot to lose by trying on different lenses.

YOU'VE BEEN ENTERING THE EMPATHY STEP THINKING YOU ALREADY KNOW YOUR WHAT'S MAKING IT HARD FOR YOUR CHILD TO MEET AN EXPECTATION
As you read earlier, it's common for adults to be incorrect in their assumptions about what's making it hard

for a child to meet an expectation. If you enter the Empathy step quite certain that you already know his concern, you're at risk for perfunctory drilling and/or for steering the ship toward a predetermined destination. But you still won't have the information you need to solve the problem.

YOU'VE BEEN ENTERING PLAN B WITH A PREORDAINED SOLUTION

It's fine to have some ideas for how a problem can be solved, but it's technically impossible to know what the solution is until you've identified the concerns of both parties. Remember, the reference point for all solutions is the degree to which it addresses the concerns of both parties.

YOU'VE BEEN AGREEING TO SOLUTIONS THAT AREN'T REALISTIC AND MUTUALLY SATISFACTORY

Before you sign off on a solution, make sure you and your child have given thought to whether the solution under consideration is truly realistic (meaning both parties can reliably follow through on what they're agreeing to do) and mutually satisfactory (meaning the concerns of both parties have truly and logically been addressed). If there's doubt about whether a solution is realistic and mutually satisfactory, you'll want to continue the discussion until you and your child agree on a solution that comes closer to the mark.

YOU'VE BEEN TRYING TO BAKE THE CAKE WITHOUT ONE OF THE THREE KEY INGREDIENTS

Each of the three ingredients, each step, is indispensable in the collaborative resolution of a problem. If you skip the Empathy step, whatever solution you come up with will (a) be uninformed and (b) only address your concerns. Those solutions tend not to work very well. Case in point:

> **ADULT:** I want to make sure you get your homework done before soccer practice from now on because if you don't do your homework before soccer practice it doesn't get done. How can we work that out?
> **KID:** Huh?

As you now know, the Define Adult Concerns step involves entering your concern or perspective into consideration. Make sure you don't enter a solution rather than a concern in this step, causing Plan B to morph into Plan A. Let's see what that looks like:

> **ADULT** (with a good introduction to the unsolved problem): I've noticed that it's difficult for you to complete your homework on days that you have soccer practice. What's up?
> **KID:** Well, I'm really tired when I get home from soccer practice, and then by the time we get through with dinner it's really late.
> **ADULT** (using good reflective listening): So, you're

really tired when you get home from soccer practice and it's really late after we finish dinner.

KID: Yeah, and I always just want to get up early the next morning and do the homework, but then I'm really tired in the morning, too.

ADULT (using more reflective listening): Ah, so you always think you'll get up to do it in the morning, but you're too tired in the morning, too.

KID: Yeah.

ADULT (checking in to find out if there's anything more): Anything else I should know about why it's hard for you to do your homework on the days you have soccer practice?

KID: No, that's it.

ADULT (entering a solution rather than a concern): Well, my concern is that if you're too tired after soccer practice and you're too tired to do the homework the next morning, then you need to do the homework before soccer practice.

KID: I don't want to do it before soccer practice! I'm tired when I get home from school and I need some time to chill!

Many adults manage to get through the first two steps of Plan B, but then skip the Invitation step and impose a solution anyway. Sometimes this is because the adults still can't fathom that a child might be able to collaborate on a realistic and mutually satisfactory solution. Most often, it's just a bad habit. Here's what

that would look like, continuing with the soccer practice unsolved problem:

> **ADULT** (this time entering a concern in the Define
> Adult Concerns step): I think I understand. Well, my
> concern is that if you're too tired to do your home-
> work after soccer, and too tired to do it early the
> next morning, then it ends up not getting done, and
> that's starting to affect your grades in a lot of your
> classes.
>
> **KID**: I know.
>
> **ADULT** (skipping the Invitation and heading straight
> into a unilateral solution): So, I've decided that if the
> homework isn't completely done before soccer prac-
> tice then you can't go to soccer practice.
>
> **KID**: What?!
>
> **ADULT** (using one of the classic rationales for Plan A):
> I'm doing this for your own good.
>
> **KID**: Well, that's a crappy idea and I'm not doing it!
>
> **ADULT**: Watch your tone, young man . . .

**THE EMPATHY STEP NEVER GOT ROLLING BECAUSE YOUR KID'S FIRST
RESPONSE TO THE UNSOLVED PROBLEM WAS "I DON'T KNOW" OR SILENCE**
As you read in the previous chapter, this causes many
people to get stuck in the Plan B mud. Remember,
your best initial strategy is to give the child some
time to think. Wording unsolved problems according to the guidelines can also reduce the likelihood

of "I don't know" and silence, so you may want to double-check your wording. Doing Plan B proactively so your child isn't surprised by your desire to have a discussion—and giving some advance notice of the topic—can reduce the likelihood of "I don't know" and silence as well. But if you're in good shape on all those counts and you still find yourself dealing with "I don't know" or silence, you'll need to figure out what the "I don't know" or silence means. Here's the short list of possibilities:

- It's possible he really doesn't know what's making it hard to meet a particular expectation. Perhaps you've never inquired before. Perhaps he's never given the matter any thought. Perhaps he's become so accustomed to having his concerns dismissed that he hasn't given any thought to his concerns for a very long time. Proactive Plan B will provide him with the opportunity to give the matter some thought, so long as you're not talking while he's trying to think. A lot of adults aren't comfortable with the silence that can occur as a kid is thinking. Remember, if you're talking while your kid is trying to think, you'll make it harder for him, thereby reducing your chances of gathering information. He may also need some of the reassurance that you read about in the previous chapter—reassurance that you're not mad, that he's not in trouble, that you're not going to tell him what to do, and that you truly just want to understand.

- He's had so much Plan A in his life that he's still betting on the Plan A horse. You'll have to reassure him that you're not riding that horse anymore. By the way, mere reassurance about that may not get the job done. The proof is in the pudding.

- He thinks he's in trouble. As discussed previously, history has taught a lot of kids that the raising of a problem means they're in hot water and that the boom is about to be lowered. You'll have to prove otherwise. By the way, this issue sometimes necessitates a Plan B discussion of its own, so you can learn as much as possible about the ways in which "problem solving" still feels like "you're in trouble" to your child.

- He may have some things to say that he knows you don't want to hear, and he thinks if he says these things, it'll cause a fight. Your goal in the Empathy step is to suspend your emotional response to what your child is saying, knowing that if you react emotionally to what you're hearing you won't end up hearing anything.

- He forgot or didn't understand what you asked. If he doesn't verbalize this, his facial expression may provide some hints. You can always inquire: "Do you remember my question?" or "Do you understand what I'm asking?"

- He's having trouble putting his thoughts into words. Some clarification might help here: "Do you know what you want to say but you're having trouble finding the words to say it? Or do you not know what you want to say?"

- He's buying time. A lot of kids say, "I don't know," instead of "Umm," or "Give me a second," or "Let me think about that a minute." Since you're not in a rush, you'll be able to give him a second and let him think about it a minute.

If, after you've given your kid the chance to think, you become convinced that he really has no idea what his concern is or is simply unable to put his thoughts into words, your best option is to do some educated guessing or hypothesis testing. Suggest a few possibilities, based on experience, and see if any resonate. Here's an example of educated guessing:

ADULT: I've noticed that you've been having difficulty taking your new medicine. What's up?
KID: I don't know.
ADULT: Well, let's think about it. There's no rush.
KID (after ten seconds): I really don't know.
ADULT: Take your time. Let's see if we can figure it out.
KID (after another five seconds): I really don't know.
ADULT: OK. You know we've run into this problem a

few times before with other medicines. Should we think about what it's been before?

KID: I can't remember.

ADULT: Well, sometimes it looks like you're having trouble swallowing the pill. Is that it?

KID: No.

ADULT: Sometimes it makes you sick to your stomach. Is that the problem now?

KID: Um, no.

ADULT: Does it bother you that you have to take it at school and the other kids see you going down to the nurse?

KID: Yes!

ADULT: Ah, so that's it. Anything else that we're not thinking of?

KID: I don't think so.

As you're in the midst of hypothesizing, bear in mind that you're proposing possibilities rather than divining the kid's concern. Here's what "divining" sounds like:

ADULT: I've noticed that you've been having difficulty taking your new medicine. What's up?

KID: I don't know.

ADULT: I think it's because you're having trouble swallowing the pill. I thought we were over that, but I guess not.

YOU GOT STUCK IN THE EMPATHY STEP BECAUSE YOU HAD TROUBLE DRILLING

It's not always easy to know what to say to keep your kid talking so you can get the information you're seeking, and there are some things kids say in response to "What's up?" that can be especially vexing. Some examples:

> **ADULT:** I've noticed you've been struggling a lot on your homework lately. What's up?
>
> **KID:** It's boring.
>
> **ADULT** (trying to drill a little): What's boring about it?
>
> **KID:** It's just boring.
>
> **ADULT** (still trying to drill): Well, can you tell me some of the assignments that you're finding boring?
>
> **KID:** My mind is a complete blank.

> **ADULT:** I've noticed you haven't been eating what I've been making for dinner lately. What's up?
>
> **KID:** I don't like it.
>
> **ADULT** (trying to drill): What don't you like about it?
>
> **KID:** It doesn't taste good.
>
> **ADULT** (still trying to drill): Well, can you tell me what doesn't taste good?
>
> **KID:** It just doesn't taste good.

When initial attempts at drilling don't strike oil, you may be inclined to abandon the well. Hang in there. You always have educated guessing or hypothesis testing as a last resort. Again, your best default drilling option, though, is reflective listening: simply saying back to the child whatever he just said, accompanied by a clarifying statement. Let's see what this drilling strategy (and others) might look like in situations in which it appears the well is dry. These dialogues don't take you all the way through Plan B; they focus solely on "drilling perseverance" (and the drilling strategy, in parentheses, that's being used):

ADULT: I've noticed you've been struggling a lot on your homework lately. What's up?

KID: It's boring.

ADULT (trying to drill a little, using Strategy #2): What's boring about it?

KID: It's just boring.

ADULT (using Strategy #2): Can you tell me what assignments you're finding boring?

KID: My mind is a complete blank.

ADULT (not abandoning the well and trying to help the kid get back into the moment, using Strategy #4): Hmm. So, when you're sitting there trying to do your homework, what are you thinking?

KID: I'm thinking it's boring.

ADULT (Strategies #1 and #4): Ah, you're thinking it's boring. What else are you thinking?

KID: I'm thinking I don't understand it.

ADULT (Strategy #2): What part are you thinking you don't understand?

KID: The math. I just don't get it.

ADULT: OK, let's talk about the parts of the math that you're not understanding . . .

Of course, the conversation would continue from there . . . but way to hang in there! Let's try another:

ADULT: I've noticed you haven't been eating what I've been making for dinner lately. What's up?

KID: I don't like it.

ADULT (using Strategy #2): What don't you like about it?

KID: I just don't like it.

ADULT (using Strategy #1): You just don't like it. Can you say more about that?

KID: It just doesn't taste good.

ADULT (sticking with Strategy #1): Ah, it just doesn't taste good. What do you mean?

KID: I don't know.

ADULT (not abandoning the well and using drilling Strategy #3): You know, I noticed that some nights you eat what I make and some nights you don't. Are there some things I make that you like and some things I make that you don't?

KID: I like pasta.

ADULT: Yes, I've noticed that you do like pasta. But I think there are other things I make that you eat.

KID: Like what?

ADULT: Rice.

KID: Oh, yeah, rice. But when you put all that stuff in it, like nuts, and those little slices of orange, it's disgusting.

ADULT: Is there anything else I make that you like?

KID: No.

ADULT: Is there anything I make that you especially don't like? I mean, besides the rice with the nuts and mandarin oranges in it.

KID: Well, I kinda like your meatballs, but that's it. And I don't like the vegetables . . . except corn on the cob.

ADULT: I'm glad we're figuring out what you like and don't like. That'll help us solve this problem.

YOUR KID VERBALIZED HIS CONCERN OR PERSPECTIVE IN THE EMPATHY STEP, BUT YOU DIDN'T BELIEVE HIM

While it's conceivable that your kid's first stab at identifying and articulating his concern may not be spot on (after all, he may not have given his concerns much thought until you asked), a lot of adults are quick to view a kid's concern as wrong or untrue. But the last thing you'd want to do is dismiss his concern or, worse, tell him you think he's lying. That approach is useful only for getting him to stop talking to you. I've found that most of the concerns that adults thought were wrong or untrue actually had a kernel of truth to them. If you're drilling well, you'll give your kid the opportunity to clarify his concerns.

When adults tell me they think a kid is lying in the Empathy step, it's often because the adult isn't inquiring about a specific unsolved problem but rather about a *behavior* someone saw the kid exhibit, usually setting the stage for an exercise in *grilling* rather than drilling. Here's what that sounds like (notice the adult isn't really doing the Empathy step):

PARENT: I heard from your teacher, Ms. Adams, that you hit Jovan on the playground.

KID: I did not. She's lying.

PARENT: Now, why would Ms. Adams lie about that?

KID: I don't know, but she is. I didn't hit him. He hit me.

PARENT: That's not what she said.

KID: Well, she's wrong.

PARENT: She said she saw it with her own eyes!

KID: Then she's blind, 'cuz I didn't hit him. He hit me. Why don't you believe me?

Whether or not the kid is telling the truth is one issue (we all know how unreliable eyewitness accounts can be). But trying to get to the bottom of a specific *incident* is beside the point anyway, because what happened in a specific incident isn't nearly as important as solving the chronic problem of the kid and Jovan having difficulty getting along on the playground.

YOUR KID SAID HE DIDN'T CARE ABOUT YOUR CONCERN, SO YOUR EN-
THUSIASM FOR PLAN B DISSIPATED RAPIDLY

Don't be insulted that he doesn't care about your concern. Let's face it, you may not actually care that much
about his. The good news is that he doesn't really have
to care about your concern; he just has to take it into
account as you pursue a mutually satisfactory solution
together. He'll start trying to address your concerns
not too long after you start trying to address his. Here's
an example:

> **PARENT:** Hector, I've noticed that it's been difficult for
> you to come in for dinner when you're playing outside.
> What's up?
>
> **HECTOR:** You always make me come in when I'm in the
> middle of something fun.
>
> **PARENT:** Ah, you're always in the middle of something
> fun. Is there anything else about my calling you in for
> dinner that's hard for you?
>
> **HECTOR:** No. I just don't want to come in if I'm in the
> middle of a fun game.
>
> **PARENT:** I understand. The thing is, you're almost
> always in the middle of something fun when I call you
> in for dinner, and it's really important to me that we
> eat dinner together as a family.
>
> **HECTOR:** I don't care if we eat dinner together as a family.
>
> **PARENT:** Um . . . OK. Well, I guess it's probably more
> important to me that we eat together than it is to

you. But I'm thinking that if we could get the problem solved in a way that works for both of us, then we could stop arguing about it.

YOUR KID DIDN'T HAVE ANY IDEAS FOR SOLUTIONS

Hopefully you had some ideas. Remember, it's not his job to solve the problem; it's the job of the problem-solving partners: you and him. So, if your kid truly has no ideas, it's fine for you to offer some proposals, so long as you don't end up imposing your will in the process. This is discussed further in chapter 9.

PLAN B NEVER GOT OFF THE GROUND BECAUSE YOUR KID BLEW UP THE MINUTE YOU STARTED TALKING OR WAS TOO HYPERACTIVE TO SIT STILL FOR THE CONVERSATION

If your child becomes agitated the instant you try to initiate Proactive Plan B, many of the factors discussed in this chapter could be coming into play, and many of the remedies you've read about may help. Of course, there are other factors that could be interfering. For example, it's possible that your child lacks some skills crucial for participating in Plan B. That topic is covered fairly extensively in the next chapter. But there are some kids whose fuses are so short, who are so irritable and unhappy, or so hyperactive and/or inattentive, that they can't engage in the conversation. In those instances, it's worth considering whether medication might provide some relief and make problem solving more feasible. Some kids won't be able to participate in Plan B without the aid of medication. This topic is discussed more fully in the next chapter as well.

YOU'RE TOO EXHAUSTED OR TOO SICK OF YOUR CHILD OR TOO SCARED OF YOUR CHILD TO GIVE THIS A TRY

We have to figure out how to get your energy back. I've seen the approach described in this book accomplish just that. Relationships recover as caregivers begin to see a child's difficulties through more accurate, more compassionate eyes. Communication is renewed as a kid feels heard and legitimized. Concerning behaviors diminish as problems are solved and caregivers respond to a child's difficulties in a less punitive, less adversarial manner. The kid is less scary. The caregivers feel more empowered. The energy, compassion, and optimism come back.

But it's also the case that some caregivers need to focus on themselves, too. They need to find ways to spend time away from the child and recharge and find ways to focus on other aspects of life besides the child. Mental health clinicians, support groups, social service agencies, spouses, relatives, and friends can sometimes be of help.

• • •

Debbie was eager to return to her Plan B discussion with Jennifer. The day after her first try, Debbie approached Jennifer during breakfast again.

"Jennifer, do you remember what we were talking about yesterday morning?"

Jennifer seemed annoyed to be interrupted. "Yeah."

"Do you think we could finish solving the problem?"

"No."

Against her better judgment, Debbie tried again. "I was kind of hoping we could finish solving the problem."

The wooden look on Jennifer's face was familiar. "I'm not solving the problem."

Now things were going the way Debbie had anticipated they would the first time. She tried reflective listening. "You're not solving the problem."

"I'm not solving the problem!" yelled Jennifer, slamming her glass down on the table. "And I'm not talking about it either!"

Debbie quickly went into de-escalation mode. "OK." She began loading dishes into the dishwasher.

After a two-minute silence, Jennifer said, "I'll talk about it later."

Debbie was tempted to ask when "later" might be but thought better of it. She decided to wait it out.

Jennifer finished her waffles, put her glass and plate in the sink, and began walking to her bedroom. Debbie took a chance. "Let me know when you want to talk about it again."

Jennifer kept walking.

That afternoon, Debbie was talking with Kevin in the kitchen while Kevin made chili. Jennifer came into the kitchen.

"I think we should have a schedule," she announced.

Kevin, thinking she was talking about the dinner he was cooking, said, "Oh, I make my chili about every other week."

Jennifer had little tolerance for being misunderstood. "I wasn't talking about your f—ing chili!"

Kevin had little tolerance for profanity. Debbie saw where this was heading and intervened as Kevin was turning around to respond. "A schedule for what, honey?"

"For the TV," said Jennifer.

"For what?" said Kevin, still irked at Jennifer's earlier response.

"Forget about it!" yelled Jennifer.

"Whoa, hold on," said Debbie, shooting her "back-off" look at Kevin. "I want to hear your idea about the schedule for the TV."

"Not in here," said Jennifer, glaring at Kevin.

"How about in your room?" Debbie suggested. She and Jennifer settled themselves in Jennifer's bedroom. "Tell me your idea," said Debbie when they were both sitting down.

"I think there should be a schedule so me and Riley don't fight about what to watch on TV."

"Tell me more," said Debbie.

"Like, he could have a certain hour every day that he could watch *SportsCenter* and I could have an hour to watch my shows."

"I think that might be a great idea," said Debbie, who couldn't remember the last time Jennifer had proposed a solution to anything without screaming. "Shall I ask Riley if he'd be OK with that idea?"

Jennifer was silent. Debbie continued. "Because we'd want to make sure the idea works for him, too."

"Well, that's my solution," said Jennifer.

"Oh, I'm betting he would like the idea," Debbie reassured. "I just want to make sure."

"That's my idea, whether he likes it or not."

"Well, how about I found out if he likes it, and we can take it from there?"

Jennifer seemed finished with the conversation.

"Thanks for telling me your idea," said Debbie. "I'm glad you thought about it."

Jennifer was now distracted by her laptop. *Looks like the conversation is over*, thought Debbie.

Debbie went back out into the kitchen. "We have a very interesting daughter," she said to Kevin.

"I don't like her swearing at us," said Kevin.

"Me either," said Debbie, sitting down at the kitchen table. "But if I have to tolerate some swearing so she'll talk to us, I'll make that trade. Talking is more important to me right now."

"She's talking?"

"A little," Debbie said and smiled. "I'm starting to think there's a lot going on in that head of hers that we don't know much about."

Later, it dawned on Debbie that she hadn't talked with Sandra all weekend. She called, excited to share the latest Jennifer developments, but when Sandra answered the phone she knew immediately that something was wrong. Sandra told her that Frankie had hit her in the mouth, hard, and run away. This wasn't the first time Debbie had heard that Frankie had hit his mom, and Frankie's hitting was in a different league compared to Jennifer's.

"I don't know what to do," said Sandra.

"What was he mad about?"

"I told him the new in-home therapist was coming tomorrow. He got pissed about that. Then I got pissed 'cuz I'm sick of having these people in my house telling me what to do when it doesn't do me any damn good anyway. Then I told him that the in-home therapist wouldn't have to come if he'd just get his damn act together and that he was going to get me fired from my damn job. Then he hit me. I guess he wanted me to shut up."

"Where is he now?" asked Debbie.

"I don't know," said Sandra. "I'm betting he's not coming home tonight."

Debbie was at a loss. "Do you want me to come over? Do you want to meet somewhere?"

"I don't want you to see my lip."

"It won't bother me," said Debbie.

"I'll be OK." There was a long pause. "I don't want to live this way anymore," said Sandra, her voice breaking.

9

THE QUESTIONS

We've covered a lot of territory up to this point. And while many of your questions about solving problems collaboratively may already have been answered, it's possible many more have arisen. Time to get those questions answered. There's some repetition in this chapter, too . . . good to make sure the important points don't get overlooked.

QUESTION: If I'm using Plan B, how will my child be held accountable—you know, take responsibility—for her actions?

ANSWER: For too many people, the phrases "hold the child accountable" and "make them take responsibility" are really codes for "punishment." And many people believe (you read about this in chapter 5) that if the punishments a child has already received for their concerning behaviors haven't put an end to these behaviors, it must be because the punishments didn't cause the child enough pain. So, they add more pain. In my experience, kids with concerning behaviors have had more pain added to their lives than most people experience in a lifetime. If pain were going to work, it would have worked a long time ago. If a kid is getting their concerns on the table, taking yours into account, and working collaboratively toward solutions that work for both of you, and therefore the frequency and intensity of challenging episodes are being reduced, then you can rest assured that she's being held accountable and taking responsibility for their actions.

QUESTION: So, I can still set limits?

ANSWER: Absolutely. Remember, you're setting limits whether you're using Plan A or Plan B. With Plan A you're setting limits by imposing your will. You're also slamming the door on understanding and addressing your kid's concerns, increasing the likelihood of adversarial interactions with your child, pressing ahead with uninformed solutions, not solving problems durably, and not enhancing skills. With Plan B, you're setting limits by engaging your child in collaboratively solving the problem that was making it difficult for her to meet your expectations. When you set limits using Plan B, you're learning about what's getting in your child's way, decreasing adversarial interactions, working together on solutions that are realistic and mutually satisfactory, enhancing the skills she's lacking (and perhaps learning some new skills yourself), and solving problems durably. The hardest thing about Plan B is becoming good at it.

QUESTION: Does Plan B make it clear to my child that I disapprove of her behavior?

ANSWER: Yes. The mere fact that you're talking to your child about the problems that are causing her behavior makes it quite clear that things need to be different. By the way, a lot of the concerning behaviors you disapprove of occur in the context of using Plan A. If you're not relying on Plan A and are proactively solving problems with Plan B, the concerning behaviors that go along with Plan A will subside as well.

QUESTION: What about the real world? What if my kid has a "Plan A" boss someday?

ANSWER: A Plan A boss is a problem to be solved. Which skill set is more important for life in the real world: the blind adherence to authority taught with Plan A, or identifying and articulating one's concerns, taking others' concerns into account, and working toward solutions that are realistic and mutually satisfactory with Plan B? If kids are completely dependent on the imposition of adult will to do the right thing, then what will they do when adults aren't around to impose their will? My friend Tony Wagner has written some very influential books—including *The Global Achievement Gap: Why Even Our Best Schools Don't Teach the New Survival Skills Our Children Need—and What We Can Do About It*—about the skills kids are going to need to lead productive, adaptive lives in the future. Foremost among those skills: collaboration and problem solving. Blind adherence to authority didn't make the list.

QUESTION: Aren't safety issues best addressed with Plan A?
ANSWER: It depends on the situation. As you've read, in emergent safety situations (e.g., your child is about to step in front of a speeding car), imposition of adult will (yanking on her arm) may make perfect sense. With other emergent safety issues (e.g., your child has a chair over her head and is threatening to throw it), de-escalating things may actually make more sense than Plan A. But here's the most important point: if your child is exhibiting chronic safety problems—perhaps she's *frequently* darting in front of moving cars in a parking lot—then Proactive Plan B is likely to be your best long-term option for solving that problem. Here's what that sounds like:

> **PARENT** (initiating the Empathy step): Chris, I've noticed that it's a little hard for you to stay next to me when we're in parking lots. What's up?
> **CHRIS:** I don't know.

PARENT: Well, let's think about it a second. What's so hard about staying next to me when we're in the parking lot?

CHRIS: Um . . . I guess I'm just really excited about getting into the store.

PARENT: Yes, I've noticed that you're very excited about getting into the store. Is there any other reason you think it's hard to stay next to me?

CHRIS: Um . . . I don't like it when you hold my hand. That's for babies.

PARENT: Ah, yes, I've noticed that, too. Anything else you can think of that would help me understand why you're having trouble staying next to me in the parking lot?

CHRIS: Not really.

PARENT: OK. So, you're having trouble staying next to me because you're really excited to get into the store and you don't like it when I hold your hand. Yes?

CHRIS: Uh-huh.

PARENT (initiating the Define Adult Concerns step): I understand. My concern is that it's dangerous for you to run in front of cars, and that's what happens if I don't hold your hand. And if I see that you're about to run in front of a car, I have to grab you so you don't get hurt, and then we get mad at each other. Know what I mean?

CHRIS: Yup.

PARENT (initiating the Invitation step): I wonder if there's a way for us to keep you from running in front of cars in the parking lot so you don't get hurt without me holding your hand. Do you have any ideas?

CHRIS: Um . . . we could not go into parking lots.

PARENT: That's an idea. The thing is, sometimes we have to go into parking lots, like to go food shopping or to the drugstore. So, I don't know if we can stay away from parking lots completely. But I bet there's some way we could be in parking lots without my having to worry about you running in front of cars and without me holding your hand. What do you think?

CHRIS: You could leave me home with Grammy.

PARENT: I could, sometimes. But Grammy can't always look after you when I'm out doing errands.

CHRIS: I could hold your belt loop.

PARENT: You could hold my belt loop. That would be better than me holding your hand?

CHRIS: Yes. Holding hands is for babies.

PARENT: You'd hold my belt loop even if you were really excited about getting into the store?

CHRIS: Yes.

PARENT: What if I'm wearing something that doesn't have a belt loop?

CHRIS: Um . . . I guess I could just hold on to whatever you're wearing.

PARENT: I think that idea could work very well. Can I remind you to hold my belt loop before we get out of the car?

CHRIS: Yes.

PARENT: But sometimes you get mad when I remind you that parking lots are dangerous.

CHRIS: That's because I already know parking lots are dangerous. I only get mad if you're screaming at me to hold your hand.

PARENT: I'm screaming at you because you're . . . you know what? If you and I agree that you're going to hold my belt loop in the parking lot from now on, then it won't matter why I was screaming at you.

CHRIS: What if you forget not to scream at me?

PARENT: I'm going to try very hard not to. If I slip, can you remind me?

CHRIS: Yup.

PARENT: This plan works for you?

CHRIS: Yup.

PARENT: It works for me, too. And if our solution doesn't work, we'll talk about it some more and think of another solution.

Often when parents refer to "safety issues" they're referring to what their child is doing (hitting, throwing things) *in the midst of a challenging episode.* Again, since a high percentage of challenging episodes are precipitated by an adult using Plan A, using Plan B instead of Plan A should make a major dent in the frequency of safety issues.

QUESTION: Everything I'm reading makes good sense to me, and I get the importance of being proactive. But what if I should find myself in the middle of a challenging episode?

ANSWER: If you should find yourself in the middle of a challenging episode, it's a pretty sure bet you're using Plan A. The best advice is to defuse and de-escalate the situation so as to keep everyone safe. If you're lucky and your child is still, at that moment, capable of rational thought, then Emergency Plan B is an option. If not, then one viable option is to use Plan C at that moment and use Proactive Plan B at the next possible opportunity to solve the problem that set in motion the concerning behaviors in the first place. Concerning behaviors provide very important information about unsolved problems you may have missed or failed to prioritize. That's perhaps the only useful thing about such behaviors: they let you know there's still work to be done to prevent the same problem from recurring.

QUESTION: I don't have time to use Plan B. It takes too long.

ANSWER: You may want to take a look at how long it's taking you to deal with the concerning behaviors that are caused by Plan A. Most people find that concerning behaviors always take longer to deal with than Plan B would have taken to prevent them. Unsolved problems always take more time than solved problems. Doing something that isn't working always takes more time than doing something that will work. If you and your child are collaborating on durable solutions, then the amount of time you're spending using Plan B will decrease over time as problems are solved.

QUESTION: I'm not that quick on my feet. I can't always decide what Plan to use on the spur of the moment.
ANSWER: It's only in the heat of the moment that you have to be quick on your feet. Another of the many reasons that being proactive is far preferable.

QUESTION: I started using Plan B with my daughter, and she talked! In fact, she talked so much and I gathered so much information that I started becoming overwhelmed with all the problems we need to solve! Help!
ANSWER: It's true, sometimes Plan B opens the information floodgates, and you find out there were even more problems to solve than those you identified on the ALSUP. While that can feel overwhelming, it's good that you're now aware of all of those unsolved problems. Your goal is to add any new unsolved problems to your list, perhaps reprioritize, and continue the mission of solving one problem at a time.

QUESTION: So, I'm not a failure if I don't make it through all three steps of Plan B in one sitting?
ANSWER: Not at all! If you didn't make it past the Empathy step in the first attempt at Plan B, but you now understand what's making it hard for your kid to meet a particular expectation, I'd say you've been

quite successful. Just make sure you follow up with the next two steps before too much time passes.

QUESTION: What if my child and I agree on a solution and then she won't do what she agreed to?

ANSWER: As you've read, that's usually a sign that the solution wasn't as realistic and mutually satisfactory as you may have first thought. That's not a catastrophe, just a reminder that the first solution to a problem often doesn't get the job done. Remember, effective problem solving tends to be incremental; good solutions are usually variants of the solutions that preceded them. It's also important to remember that Plan B isn't an exercise in wishful thinking. Both parties need to be able to follow through on their part of the solution. If your child isn't following through, it's probably not because she won't but because she can't. By the way, kids aren't the only ones who don't follow through on unrealistic solutions; adults aren't very good at it either.

QUESTION: I did it! My child and I did Plan B together and we solved our first problem, and the solution seems to be working so far. Now what?

ANSWER: Well done! You're on your way to having the problem durably solved, though it sounds like you recognize that the solution may not stand the test of time. What's next? Move on to another high-priority unsolved problem, and then another. Along the way, be sure to look in the rearview mirror to take stock of the progress you're making.

QUESTION: I understand how Plan B helps me solve problems with my child. But how are my child's lagging skills going to get taught?

ANSWER: Great question. The reality is that there aren't great strategies for directly teaching many of the lagging skills on the ALSUP. However, there is a great technology for enhancing those skills: Plan B. When you're collaboratively and proactively solving problems, you are indirectly teaching skills.

In other words, many skills are enhanced just by doing Plan B with your child, irrespective of the specific unsolved problem you're working on. In the Empathy step, kids practice reflecting on their concerns and expressing those concerns in ways that other people can hear and understand. In the Define Adult Concerns step, kids practice listening to another person's concerns (what many of us refer to as empathy), taking another person's perspective, and appreciating how their behavior is affecting others. In the Invitation step, kids get practice at considering a range of solutions to a problem, considering the likely outcomes of those solutions, and shifting from a solution that only works for them to a solution that will work for other people, too. Lots of skills are being taught and practiced with Plan B; and remember: it's not just the kid who's getting good at those skills.

Plan B also helps your child build a repertoire of solutions. Here's what I mean: Because I fly frequently, I am commonly faced with the problem that a delayed or canceled flight will prevent me from reaching my intended destination in time for a speaking engagement. Now, no one has ever sat me down and provided me with direct instruction on what to do if my flight is canceled or delayed. I learned through experience, and those experiences (successful and not so successful) provide the foundation for my "what to do if your flight is delayed or canceled" repertoire. There may be alternate flights on the same airline. There may be alternate flights on a different airline. There may be alternate flights to nearby destinations. There are rental cars. There are trains. Don't most people have the skills to apply past experiences to problems they face in the present? Yes. But, as evidenced by the meaningful number of fellow passengers I've seen exhibit concerning behavior when their flights are delayed or canceled, apparently not all.

By solving problems collaboratively with your child, you are helping your child build a repertoire of solutions. By solving problems proactively, you may be helping your child access solutions that are already in her repertoire but that, when she's heated up, she's unable to access.

QUESTION: What's the role of medication in helping kids with behavioral challenges?

ANSWER: There are some kids who are so hyperactive, impulsive, inattentive, irritable, anxious, and/or have such a short fuse and are so emotionally reactive that it's extremely difficult for them to participate in Plan B until these issues have been satisfactorily addressed. If any (or many) of these issues are making participation in Plan B difficult, then presumably they're making other aspects of life difficult as well. These are issues for which medication can sometimes be helpful.

Many parents have an instant negative reaction to the idea of medicating their child, and for good reason. These days, too many kids are medicated unnecessarily, too many are on too much medication, and too many are on medication for things medication does not address well. Psychotropic medication isn't always prescribed with the level of expertise, care, and diligence it deserves. But medication can be helpful for some of the factors contributing to concerning behavior and make it more possible for some kids to participate in Plan B. So, while a conservative approach to medication is totally appropriate, you may not want to rule out the possibility completely. In some kids, medication is an indispensable component of treatment.

Deciding whether to medicate one's child *should* be difficult. You'll need a lot of information, much more than is provided here, especially about side effects. Some medications that are commonly prescribed for kids haven't been approved for use with kids, nor have many been studied extensively in use with children and adolescents, especially with regard to their long-term side effects. Your doctor should help you weigh the anticipated benefits of medication with the potential risks so you can make educated decisions. Although it's important to have faith in the doctor's expertise, it's equally important that you feel comfortable with the treatment plan they propose, or at least that you're comfortable with the balance between benefits and risks. If you are not comfortable with or confident in the information you've been given, you need more information. If your doctor doesn't have the time or expertise to provide you with more information, you need a new doctor. Medical treatment is not something to fear, but it needs to be implemented competently and compassionately and monitored continuously. Ultimately, what you'll need most of all is a competent, clinically savvy, attentive, and available prescribing doctor. You'll want one who:

- Takes the time to get to know you and your child, listens to you, and is familiar with treatment options that have nothing to do with a prescription pad

- Knows that a diagnosis provides little useful information about your kid

- Understands that there are some things medication doesn't treat well at all

- Has a good working knowledge of the potential side effects of medication and their management

- Makes sure that you—and your kid, if it's appropriate—understand each medication and its anticipated benefits and potential side effects and interactions with other medications

- Is willing to devote sufficient time to monitoring your child's progress carefully and continuously over time

When children have a poor response to medication, it is often because one of the foregoing elements was missing from their treatment.

A discreet approach to medication is also recommended. A lot of kids aren't eager for their classmates to know that they're receiving medication to address emotional or behavioral issues. If there's no way to keep your child's classmates in the dark, it's often necessary to educate the classmates about individual differences (asthma, allergies, diabetes, difficulty concentrating, low frustration tolerance, etc.) that may require medicinal treatment. On the other hand, while there's a temptation for parents to avoid doing so, I typically encourage parents to keep relevant school personnel well-informed about their child's medication. The observations and feedback of teachers are often crucial to making appropriate adjustments in medication; the goal is to work as a collaborative team.

QUESTION: If I choose to medicate my child, how long will she be on the medication?

ANSWER: That's very hard to predict. In general, the chemical benefits of medication endure only as long as the medication is taken. However, because of maturation and/or because new skills and improved relationships were developed when the medication was being prescribed, it is sometimes possible to discontinue the medication. Ultimately, the question of whether a child should remain on medication must be continuously revisited.

QUESTION: What about homeopathic and natural remedies?

ANSWER: Some parents feel better about using such remedies instead of prescribed medication, and some kids benefit from them. But it's important to apply the same standard to homeopathic and natural remedies as we would to prescribed medication. Don't stick with it if it's not helpful, or if the intervention is doing more harm than good, or if there are other interventions that might be more effective.

QUESTION: My child has significant communication delays. I'm wondering if Plan B is truly realistic for her.

ANSWER: Since all of the examples of Plan B you've read so far depict kids with half-decent communication skills, it's no wonder you're wondering. So, let's focus for a while on how one would go about solving problems collaboratively without the aid of the spoken word. The good news is that these kids are already communicating; what makes life more difficult is that they're not communicating through what is the preferred modality for many caregivers (the spoken word). But Plan B can be adjusted for kids with compromised communication skills so that you can identify unsolved problems, gather some information about the concerns related to these unsolved problems, and participate with your kid in the process of generating and evaluating solutions.

A useful reference point, by the way, is infants. Infants may have any variety of unsolved problems: hunger, difficulty being away from mom and/or dad, difficulty sleeping away from mom and/or dad, difficulty eating, difficulty digesting food, difficulty establishing a regular sleep cycle, difficulty self-soothing, difficulty dealing with the sensory world (lights, noises, heat, cold, etc.), but they don't have the words to tell us about them. They are communicating, but they are doing so in ways that don't involve spoken words. If you think about it carefully, we actually do collaborate with infants on solutions: after caregivers try to figure out what the infant is communicating and then apply solutions aimed at addressing the infant's concerns, we are completely dependent on the feedback provided by the infant to determine whether the concern has been addressed or not. All without words. If we can do that with infants, we can do that with kids (and adults) of any age who are unable or severely limited in their ability to communicate through use of the spoken word.

Let's think about what it would look like to engage a kid in solving problems collaboratively without the use of many (or any) words.

IDENTIFYING UNSOLVED PROBLEMS

The first goal remains the same: create a list of the unsolved problems that are reliably and predictably precipitating concerning behaviors. While grunting and growling and screaming are less explicit than words, they are occurring under highly specific conditions, and your observations about those conditions will help you generate a list of unsolved problems.

As an example, Roger was an adolescent boy whose expressive language skills were delayed but who was able to understand much of what was being said to him. His caregivers hadn't yet put much energy into identifying the conditions in which challenging episodes were occurring. Once they gave some thought to it, they found that his unsolved problems included being hot, being tired, feeling sick, being hungry, thinking someone was mad at him, being surprised, feeling that people were talking too much, and having difficulty with an academic task. They wrote those unsolved problems down on an index card, and whenever Roger would start to become agitated, they would recite the possibilities to him to find out which might be the cause. The adults soon memorized the items, thereby eliminating the need for the index card, and Roger eventually memorized the possibilities as well. Over time, Roger began verbalizing problems. For example, instead of screaming and pounding his fists, he'd say, "I'm hot." While this was certainly an improvement, most of the problem solving still occurred in the heat of the moment. So, the adults put some energy into identifying the specific conditions in which each of the unsolved problems was likely to occur, and then began engaging Roger in the process of coming up with solutions *ahead of time*. There was still an occasional need for figuring out what was troubling Roger in the heat of the moment, but with lots of proactive solutions in place, that need diminished greatly over time.

Of course, specific concerns such as "I'm hot" only apply to situations in which a kid is hot. It can also be useful to teach a more generic "problem vocabulary" that a kid can use across many situations to alert adults to the fact that there's a problem. An especially good phrase is "something's the matter." Having a kid *say* "something's the matter" is far preferable to having the kid *demonstrate* that something's the matter (by biting, hitting, screaming, or swearing). Teaching this phrase begins by providing the kid with direct instruction on the use of those simple words and having adults say "looks like something's the matter" whenever it looks like something's the matter. Of course, that's what's happening in the heat of the moment. It's then important for the adults to identify unsolved problems that are accounting for times when the kid is saying "something's the matter" so as to solve those problems proactively. The child won't have need of their new phrase so often as you solve the problems that were causing something to be the matter.

We adults overestimate the linguistic skills we use to let people know we're frustrated or stuck or overwhelmed. But most adults lean on a few key phrases. By teaching them to kids, we're helping to raise them to the same communication level as the rest of us.

Kia is a three-year-old girl diagnosed with an autism spectrum disorder. She was using very few words to communicate. The initial goal for Kia was the same as for Roger: find a way to establish a basic vocabulary for unsolved problems. There are various technologies that could have helped, but Kia's speech-and-language therapist chose to use Google Images to depict in pictures, placed on a laminated card, the unsolved problems that were reliably and predictably precipitating her concerning behaviors. They included being hot, being cold, being hungry, being thirsty, and something

not going the way she thought it would. Here's a repro-
duction of what that looked like:

When Kia needed to let her parents and teachers
know there was a problem, or when she began exhibiting signs of frustration, the adults would ask her to
point to the picture that best communicated what was
frustrating her. When Kia pointed to a picture, her
caregivers would verbally confirm the problem (e.g.,
"Ah, you're hungry"). Whenever Kia encountered a
problem that wasn't depicted in pictures, new pictures
were added to the "problem card." After the basic
menu of problems was established, a second laminated
card was created that depicted potential solutions cor-
responding to each unsolved problem (this is described
in the next section). The long-term goal was for Kia
to begin using words rather than pointing, and in the

meantime her frustration over having difficulty communicating diminished.

When a kid has significant communication challenges or other cognitive impairments it is crucial to give serious consideration to the words or concepts that are the absolute highest priority and that need to be taught first. The words or concepts needed for pinpointing unsolved problems or concerns, solving problems, and handling frustration should be a very high priority, because not having these words causes the kids' most concerning moments and impedes their ability to learn much else. While a vocabulary for feelings (happy, sad, mad) may seem important, such a vocabulary actually may not be a high priority because it's more important for her to communicate about the *problems* that are causing her to be sad, mad, or frustrated than to simply express that she is sad, mad, or frustrated. Communicating the cause of her feelings will give you a faster track to resolving the problem.

IDENTIFYING AND SELECTING SOLUTIONS

The same strategies that are useful for identifying unsolved problems can be applied to identifying and choosing solutions to those problems. Kia's parents created a problem-solving binder filled with laminated cards depicting in pictures potential solutions for each of the problems depicted on her "problem card." Here are some representations of what that looked like:

Being cold   Being hungry

Being thirsty   Being hot

When she signaled that she was hungry, she would turn to the card in the binder containing pictures of potential solutions to that problem. If it became apparent that additional solutions were needed, pictures of additional solutions were added. Thus, the rudimentary binder system helped Kia participate in the process of communicating not only about problems but also about potential solutions.

It's the last element—participating in the process—that is perhaps the most important for kids like Kia. Often it's assumed that kids with limited communication skills cannot participate in the process of solving problems, but this typically isn't the case. If adults automatically assume that such kids can't participate, then the kids are relegated to the sidelines as decisions are made about how their problems are to be solved. Many can, in fact, participate in Plan B, and doing so opens the door to enhanced relationships and communication with important people in their lives. Sometimes it just takes a little extra creativity and perhaps some additional resources to get Plan B rolling.

By the way, the problem-solving binder can be just as useful with kids whose communication skills are not compromised but who benefit from having a system in place to organize problems, concerns, and solutions.

A few other points before we move on. Because some solutions are applicable only to certain problems (for example, a hot dog would make good sense for the problem of being hungry but wouldn't be a great solution for most other problems), sometimes it's a good idea to teach a more general set of solutions. A high percentage of the solutions to problems encountered by human beings fall into one of three general categories: (1) ask for help, (2) meet halfway or give a little, and (3) do it a different way/change the plan. These categories can simplify things for kids whose communication skills are compromised and who may benefit from having the three possibilities depicted in pictures, as well as for kids whose communication skills are generally intact but who become easily overwhelmed by the universe of potential solutions. These three categories can be used to guide and structure the consideration of possible solutions.

First, you'll want to introduce the categories to your child at an opportune moment. Then, when you're trying to generate solutions using Plan B, use the categories as the framework for considering solutions. As with the previous examples, verbalize the words that correspond to each picture ("Ah, do it a different way") to confirm the kid's idea and encourage the use of words. Then the universe of ways in which things could be "done a different way" in order to solve the problem can be explored. Let's see what that might look like with a speaking child:

PARENT (Empathy step, using Proactive Plan B): I've noticed that you've been having difficulty going to gymnastics lately. What's up?

CHILD: I don't like my new coach.

ADULT: You don't like your new coach. You mean Ginny? How come?

CHILD: It's boring. All she has us do is stretch. That's boring.

ADULT: OK, let me make sure I've got this straight. You haven't wanted to go to gymnastics lately because it's boring, just a bunch of stretching.

CHILD: Right.

ADULT: Is that the only reason you haven't wanted to go to gymnastics lately?

CHILD: Uh-huh.

ADULT (Define Adult Concerns step): I can understand that. The thing is, you usually really like gymnastics, and you're really good at it, so I'd hate to see you give it up.

CHILD: I don't care.

ADULT: You don't care?

CHILD: Not if it's just going to be a bunch of stretching.

ADULT (Invitation step): Well, I wonder if there's a way for us to do something about your not liking all that stretching without you having to give up gymnastics completely. Do you have any ideas?

CHILD: Ginny's not going to change the way she does her class.

ADULT: You might be right about that. But let's think about our problem-solving options. I don't know if "asking for help" will solve this problem. And I can't think of how we would "meet halfway" or "give a little" on this one, especially if you think Ginny isn't going to change the way she does her class. I'm thinking this is one where we'd "try to do it a different way." What do you think?

CHILD: I don't know what a different way would be.

ADULT: Well, Ginny's not the only one who teaches that level. The main reason we picked Ginny's class is because the other class that's your level is the same time as your karate lesson. But maybe we could change karate to a different time. Then you could be in the other gymnastics class. What do you think?

Naturally, this Plan B discussion would continue until a realistic and mutually satisfactory solution has been agreed on. Not only would the problem get solved, but Plan B would help the child begin using the solution categories as a framework for generating solutions.

By the way, if your child has difficulties with language processing, a talented speech-and-language pathologist can take you much farther than the information provided here. Something worth looking into, if you haven't already.

• • •

Monday morning, Debbie was in the kitchen, having coffee and thinking about what had happened to Sandra the night before. Did Frankie come home? If he did, what happened then?

Jennifer came into the kitchen. "Good morning," said Debbie.

Jennifer did not respond—Debbie knew that she wouldn't—but set about the task of toasting her waffles. When the waffles were ready, Jennifer sat down to eat.

"Did Riley like my idea?" Jennifer asked suddenly.

"Sorry, what honey?" said Debbie.

"Did Riley like my idea?"

"Oh, you mean the idea about the TV schedule? I spoke with him very briefly about it last night. He seemed OK with the idea. He wasn't too sure what the schedule should be, but we didn't talk about it for very long."

"The schedule should be that I get to watch the TV when my two shows are on and he can watch before or after."

"Well, I can certainly mention that idea to him. Would you prefer that we discuss this all together or do you want me to discuss it with you separately?"

"Separately."

"I'm picking him up at hockey practice tonight, so I can mention your idea to him then."

"Did he have any ideas?"

"Not that I'm aware of."

"Because I thought of another one, just in case."

Debbie tried to hide her surprise. "You did?"

"That's what I just said!" Jennifer said impatiently.

"Sorry, I just wanted to make sure I heard you right. What was your other idea?"

"I could record my shows, just in case he wanted to watch sometimes while my shows are on."

"That's a great idea, Jennifer. Shall I run that one by him, too?"

"Yes, but I like the first idea better."

"I'll be sure to let him know that."

Jennifer's focus returned to her waffles. Debbie went back to her coffee, glancing occasionally at her daughter, in slight disbelief. Jennifer had revisited the discussion! She'd come up with more than one solution! She wanted to know if her brother was OK with her idea! Debbie couldn't resist the temptation . . . she got up and gave Jennifer a quick hug.

This did not go over well. "Why'd you do that?!" shouted Jennifer, immediately pushing Debbie away and stalking off to her room with her waffles. But Debbie thought she noticed the slightest hint of a smile on Jennifer's face as she departed.

"My partner," Debbie whispered when Jennifer was gone. "My problem-solving partner."

• • •

That night, Debbie was growing increasingly concerned that Sandra wasn't answering her phone. Sandra finally called at around 9:30 pm, sounding harried. Frankie hadn't come home all night, and Sandra had paged Matt, the new home-based mental health counselor. He'd come over and encouraged Sandra to call the police to help find Frankie. Just as she was about to, Frankie walked in. Sandra was sure Frankie would go ballistic when he saw Matt in the apartment, but he didn't. "He saw my lip and got really remorseful," said Sandra.

"I guess that's good," said Debbie.

Sandra related that Matt was able to get Frankie to start talking, and that Frankie told him that he was sorry he'd hit her, and that he hates his new program at school, and that the staff in the program are mean and the kids are way more screwed up than he is, and that his new medicine is making him feel really jittery.

"And Frankie told Matt that he's really sick of being in trouble all the time and that he's been smoking a lot of weed at his friend Tyler's—that's where he was last night—because that's the only thing that makes him feel better . . . and that he's really scared."

"Scared?" asked Debbie.

"Yeah, scared. He said he feels out of control . . . and like there's no one who can help him."

"Geez."

"That's what I'm sitting there thinking. I mean, the kid hasn't talked this much for like five years."

Sandra further related that Frankie had nodded when Matt asked if he was thinking about hurting himself. Then Frankie said he didn't want to talk anymore in front of Sandra, so Sandra sat in her bedroom while Matt and Frankie talked. About ten minutes later, Matt came and said he thought Frankie needed to be in the hospital.

"Oh, no," said Debbie.

"That's what I'm thinking!" said Sandra. "But Matt says Frankie's on board with the idea because there's an inpatient unit over in Amberville where they don't restrain kids or throw them in seclusion rooms. So, me and Matt and Frankie get in Matt's car and we drive over to the inpatient unit and that's where Frankie is now." Sandra paused, wincing at the pain in her lip. "Sorry, it hurts to talk."

"So, he's still there?"

"Yeah, he might be there for a week."

"I'm so sorry you had to go through all that," Debbie said. "Are you OK?"

"I'm glad he's safe," said Sandra. "So I'm kind of re- lieved." She paused. "But I'm really sad that he was going through all of that and couldn't tell me. I wish . . ." Sandra couldn't continue.

"Maybe this will be what gets things on track," said Debbie.

Sandra tried to collect herself. "I'm not getting my hopes

up. We've been through this before. We'll probably be right back at square one when he gets out."

"Maybe this time it'll be different."

When the conversation ended, Debbie sat quietly by the phone. She felt like crying, but wasn't quite able to figure out why. She couldn't decide whether to feel hopeful or helpless. How did Sandra find the strength to deal with everything she had on her plate? Why hadn't she just thrown in the towel a long time ago? Then she answered her own question. "Because it's her kid," she whispered quietly. "When it's your kid, you keep going." It was good that Frankie was finally talking to someone. She hoped the people at the hospital knew what they were doing.

She wondered about the things that were going on in Jennifer's head, things she knew nothing about. Still, after so many years of worrying and arguing and screaming, she felt the slightest glimmer of hope that she was finally getting to know that prickly, closed-book daughter of hers. She sighed. "Why does this have to be so hard?"

Debbie stood up and began walking toward her computer but then she did an abrupt about-face, bumping into Kevin, who was headed toward the refrigerator.

"Where you going?" Kevin asked.

"I was just thinking of going to see if your daughter wants me to tuck her in to bed."

"She hasn't wanted you to tuck her in for years."

"I know," said Debbie. "I think that's because I've been so caught up in who she *isn't* that I've been blowing right past who she *is*. I've let that get in the way of the most important parts of being her mother. And I don't want it to be that way anymore."

10

YOUR FAMILY

Every family has its challenges. Siblings don't always get along, parents don't always see eye to eye on things, everyone's too busy, kids are stressed about school or grades or friends, adults are stressed about work or money or trying to carve out time for themselves. Add a kid with concerning behaviors to the mix, and many families and marriages will be pushed to the brink.

Then add grandparents who remember the way they would've done things in the "good old days" and soccer or hockey coaches who are delighted to tell you how they'd handle your kid. Also add a pandemic, with the unrelenting togetherness and dramatically increased parental responsibility for academics. Life is now much more interesting than most people bargained for. Small annoyances turn into big issues, minor disagreements and stressors become major upheavals, and communication problems that might never have been noticed become glaring roadblocks.

Now add a child whose concerning behaviors are extremely aggressive and unsafe and who is highly volatile, reactive, and unstable, and "concerning behaviors" has taken on new meaning. In such cases, you've entered much more urgent territory, and safety and stability need to be your top immediate priorities. Stabilizing things often requires considering medications, as discussed in chapter 9, and always involves a lot of Plan C. (While Plan B may also play a role in creating greater stability, some kids simply aren't available for Plan B until they're more stable.) You want to do whatever you can to prevent those aggressive and unsafe outbursts, and that means taking the fuel (unsolved problems) out of the equation, at least until things have settled down a bit. Those outbursts are far more damaging to family life than almost any unmet expectation.

SIBLINGS

A child with concerning behaviors can make run-of-the-mill sibling rivalry look like a walk in the park. It's not uncommon for "ordinary" siblings to direct their greatest hostility and most savage acts toward each other. And it's not unusual for "ordinary" siblings to complain about preferential treatment and disparities in parental attention and expectations. But these issues can be magnified in families with a kid with concerning behaviors, because they may require such a disproportionate share of the parents' resources.

There are a few important themes that can help govern sibling interactions when a child with concerning behaviors is in the mix:

- All family members need to feel safe. As you just read, if your child with concerning behaviors is so volatile, reactive, and unstable that siblings feel unsafe, then stability and safety are your top priorities.

- All kids (and adults) have lagging skills and unsolved problems, some more than others. In other words, we're all working on something.

- All concerning behaviors tell us that a child is having difficulty meeting certain expectations.

- If a family member has unsolved problems, our job is to help solve those problems, collaboratively and proactively.

- Fair does not mean equal. As parents, we're going to do everything possible to make sure that each child gets what they need, which will be different for each child. Some kids need more than others.

- We know how hard it can be to have a sibling with concerning behaviors, and we're doing everything we possibly can to make things better.

If they are old enough, it is often useful to help brothers and sisters understand lagging skills and unsolved problems, how you're going about working on them, and why Plan A hasn't made things better. However, this understanding doesn't always keep kids from complaining about an apparent double standard between themselves and their sibling with concerning behaviors. Fortunately, parental attention is never distributed with 100 percent parity in any family, and parental priorities are never exactly the same for each child in any family. In your family, everyone gets what they need, which is different for everyone. In your family, you may be doing things differently for the child who needs extra help in the areas of flexibility, frustration tolerance, and problem solving, but you're also doing things differently for the other children, who have unsolved problems of their own. When siblings complain about disparities in parental expectations, it's an excellent opportunity to empathize and educate.

RILEY: How come you don't get mad at Jennifer when she swears at you? It's not fair!

DEBBIE: I know that it's hard for you to listen to her swearing. I don't like it very much either. But in our family, we try to help one another and make sure everyone gets what he or she needs. I'm trying to help Jennifer solve some frustrating problems and to help her think of different words she could use instead of swearing. That's what she needs help with.

RILEY: But swearing is wrong. You should get mad at her when she swears.

DEBBIE: Well, I don't get mad at you when I'm helping you with your math, right? That's because I don't think getting mad at you would help very much. Remember how I used to get mad at Jennifer whenever she swore? It didn't work very well, did it? It just made things worse. So, I'm doing something now that I think will eventually work better. I think it's starting to work pretty well.

RILEY: What are you going to do if I start swearing?

DEBBIE: I'd help you think of different words, too. Then again, you don't seem to have a problem with swearing, which is really good. So, it doesn't look like that's what you need my help with.

Plan B is an excellent option for dealing with disputes and disagreements between siblings. The ingredients are the same, except that the adults' role is that of Plan B facilitator. You'll still want to take it one problem at a time. Because problems between siblings tend to be highly predictable, Proactive Plan B is still far preferable to Emergency Plan B. You'll want to ensure that the concerns of both siblings are entered into consideration. ***Often this is better accomplished by doing the Empathy step in separate discussions with both siblings prior to bringing them together to discuss potential solutions.*** You'll also still want to make sure that the agreed-upon solutions truly address the concerns of both parties and are realistic and mutually satisfactory.

Over time, siblings feel better when problems are resolved through Plan B because they're seeing that their concerns are truly being heard, understood, and taken into account. Over time, they come to see their sibling with concerning behavior as more approachable and less terrifying. They appreciate being involved in the process of working toward solutions and come to recognize that you're able to handle the process in an evenhanded manner.

Here's what Plan B between two siblings looks like, with a parent as facilitator:

Empathy Step with Sibling #1 (Sibling #2 Is Not Present)

PARENT: I've noticed that you and your brother are having difficulty getting along when you're in the playroom together. What's up?

ANDREW: Caleb always plays with my toys.

PARENT: Ah, so you don't want him playing with your toys. But I thought we were keeping your toys in your bedroom and his toys in his bedroom, so I thought the toys in the playroom were for sharing.

ANDREW: Right.

PARENT: So, I don't think I understand what you mean when you say "your" toys.

ANDREW: The ones I'm playing with.

PARENT: Ah, so Caleb tries to play with the toys that you're still playing with.

ANDREW: Uh-huh.

PARENT: Does he know you're still playing with them?

ANDREW: I don't know. He doesn't ask me.

PARENT: How would he be able to tell you're still playing with them?

ANDREW: I don't know.

PARENT: Can you give me an example of a toy that you might be playing with and then he starts playing with it?

ANDREW: The cars.

PARENT: Ah, the cars. So, you'll be playing with the cars and then he'll butt in and want to play with them, too?

ANDREW: Well, I'm not exactly playing with them. But I'm not done with them yet.

PARENT: Oh, I see. So, you're not still using them, but you're also not done with them. Yes?

ANDREW: Yes.

PARENT: How would Caleb know you're not done with them if you're not still using them?

ANDREW: I don't know.

PARENT: And how much time should pass when you're not playing with them before you're through with them?

ANDREW: I don't know.

PARENT: OK, I think I understand. I'm going to talk to Caleb about this, too, because fighting over the toys is making you guys hurt each other and that's not OK in our house.

ANDREW: OK.

Empathy Step with Sibling #2 (Sibling #1 Is Not Present)

PARENT: Caleb, I've noticed that you and your brother are having difficulty getting along when you're in the playroom together. What's up?

CALEB: He won't let me play with the toys I want to play with.

PARENT: How come he won't let you play with the toys you want to play with?

CALEB: He says he's still playing with them. But he's not still playing with them! And then there's nothing for me to play with!

PARENT: So, he gets mad if you play with toys that it seems like he's not playing with anymore.

CALEB: Yes!

PARENT: So, you're not trying to play with what he's playing with right then?

CALEB: No, I'm trying to play with something else! But he says he's still playing with everything I try to play with!

PARENT: So, there's nothing left to play with.

CALEB: Uh-huh. Then he hits me when I try to play with something.

PARENT: We need to solve this problem, don't we?

CALEB: Yes, because I never get to play with anything if Andrew's around.

PARENT: I think we need to have a meeting with Andrew so we can talk about it.

Invitation Step with Siblings #1 and #2

PARENT: I've talked with both of you about the problem you've been having playing with toys together, and I thought it would be good to come up with a solution together. Andrew, you told me that sometimes you're still playing with toys even though you're not exactly using them, yes?

ANDREW: Yes.

PARENT: And Caleb, you told me that there's so many toys that Andrew is still playing with that there's nothing left for you to play with, yes?

CALEB: Uh-huh.

PARENT: I wonder if there's a way for Caleb to know what toys you're still playing with, Andrew, but still have some toys to play with himself. Do you guys have any ideas?

ANDREW: He could stay out of the room I'm playing in.

PARENT: Well, that's one idea. But if you're in the

playroom, and Caleb isn't allowed in there while you're in there, I don't know if that would be fair to Caleb.

ANDREW: But he has toys in his room! He could play with them. And then he wouldn't touch mine.

CALEB: I don't want to play with the toys in my room all the time! I want to play with the toys in the play-room sometimes!

PARENT: Any other ideas for how we could know what toys Andrew is still playing with but still have some toys for Caleb to play with?

ANDREW: I could tell him what toys I'm still playing with.

CALEB: You already do that . . . and it's everything!

PARENT: Andrew, how long does it take for you to be done playing with something?

ANDREW: I don't know.

PARENT: Like, we're sitting here talking right now. And you haven't been in the playroom since this morning. Is there anything you're still playing with in the play-room?

ANDREW: Um . . . the cars.

CALEB: No way! He hasn't been in there since this morning!

ANDREW: Yeah, but I have them set up a certain way and I don't want you to wreck 'em!

PARENT: So, I wonder what we could do about this. Caleb feels it's not fair if you're never through playing with the cars. And Caleb, Andrew would prefer that you not play with the cars if he has them set up a certain way and doesn't want you to wreck the setup. This is a hard one!

CALEB: At school, you're done playing with a toy when playtime ends.

PARENT: Hmm. So, when playtime ends, it's a fresh start on who's playing with the toys?

CALEB: Uh-huh. That's how it is at school. But not here.

PARENT: Well, maybe it could work here. Andrew, what do you think of the idea of having a time limit on how long you're still playing with toys that you haven't used in a while, like they do at school?

ANDREW: How long?

PARENT: I don't know, that's for you guys to decide. I'm wondering what you think of the idea.

ANDREW: Maybe it could work.

CALEB: I think he should be done playing with a toy as soon as he's not using it anymore.

PARENT: What do you think, Andrew?

ANDREW: That's too quick.

PARENT: Any ideas for what wouldn't be too quick?

ANDREW: Ten minutes. If I haven't used a toy for ten minutes, I'm through playing with it.

PARENT: Caleb, what do you think?

CALEB: That would give me a lot more toys to play with.

PARENT: Andrew, this could be very hard for you. Caleb would be able to play with the cars you have set up

right now because it's been a lot longer than ten minutes since you used them. Can you do that?

ANDREW: Maybe Caleb would listen to me if I asked
him not to play with the cars because I have them set
up . . . but he could play with everything else.

PARENT: Caleb, could you do that?

CALEB: Yes, if he told me. But he doesn't tell me. He
just tells me I can't play with anything!

PARENT: So, let's think about what we're deciding
here. Andrew, if you haven't used something for ten
minutes, then you're through playing with it. And
Caleb, if Andrew tells you that he's set something
up in an extra-special way, then you'll try not to play
with it. Yes?

ANDREW: Yes.

CALEB: Uh-huh.

PARENT: Well, we'll have to see how this solution
works. If it doesn't, don't start hitting each other; just
let me know so we can keep working on it.

These discussions can require a meaningful amount
of adult guidance and management. Early on, siblings
may need help listening to each other, waiting for each
other to finish talking, taking turns, not overreacting to
observations and ideas with which they don't agree, and
so forth. If they can't handle being in the same room
for the Invitation step, caregivers sometimes need to
do some "shuttle diplomacy" (going back and forth between the two parties without them having face-to-face

discussions) until some problems have been solved and the siblings have some practice and faith in the process.

By the way, in some instances the behavior of seemingly angelic siblings can begin to deteriorate just as the behavior of their behaviorally challenging brother or sister begins to improve. This is often a sign that the emotional needs of the siblings, which had been below the radar while the family dealt with the pressing issues of the child with concerning behaviors, require closer attention. In some cases, therapy may be necessary for brothers and sisters who have been traumatized by their behaviorally challenging sibling or who may be manifesting other problems that can be traced back to the old family atmosphere.

If you feel that your family needs more help working on these issues than this small section provides, a skilled family therapist can be of great assistance. If you haven't already, you may also wish to read an excellent book, *Siblings Without Rivalry*, by Adele Faber and Elaine Mazlish.

COMMUNICATION PATTERNS

A family therapist can also help when it comes to making some fundamental changes in how you communicate with your child. Dealing effectively with a kid with concerning behaviors is easier (not easy, *easier*) when there are healthy patterns of communication between the kid and their parents. When these patterns are unhealthy, dealing effectively with such a child is much harder.

For example, parents and children sometimes get into a vicious cycle, called *speculation*, of drawing erroneous conclusions about each other's motives or thoughts. Others have referred to this pattern as *psychologizing* or *mind reading*, and it can sound something like this:

> **PARENT:** The reason Oscar doesn't listen to us is that he thinks he's so much smarter than we are.

Now, it's fairly common for people to make inaccurate inferences about one another. Indeed, responding effectively to these inaccuracies, in other words, setting people straight about yourself in a manner they can hear and understand, is a real talent and requires some big-time emotion regulation and communication skills. While there are some kids who are able to respond to speculation by making appropriate, corrective statements to set the record straight ("Dad, I don't think that's true at all"), a kid with concerning behaviors may not have those skills and may therefore become extremely frustrated in the face of these inaccuracies. This is an undesirable circumstance in and of itself, but it's especially undesirable because whether Oscar thinks he's smarter than his parents isn't really the point. In fact, this topic is a detour that just distracts everyone from working collaboratively toward solutions to the unsolved problems that are setting the stage for Oscar's challenging episodes. Of course, speculation can be a two-way street. From a child's mouth, it might sound something like this:

> **OSCAR:** The only reason you guys get so mad at me so much is because you like pushing me around.

Such statements can have the same detour effect, especially when adults follow along:

> **MOTHER:** Yes, that's exactly right: our main goal in life is to push you around. I can't believe you'd say that, after all we've been through with you.
> **OSCAR:** Well, what is your main goal then?
> **FATHER:** Our main goal is to help you be normal.
> **OSCAR:** So now I'm not normal. Thank you very much, loser.
> **FATHER:** Don't you get disrespectful with me, pal.

Speculation is a no-win proposition. Solving problems collaboratively is a win-win proposition. So, let's stick to the script and, instead of *speculating* on what another family member is thinking or feeling, we'll *drill* for that information instead. That takes a lot of the guesswork and speculating out of the mix.

Another maladaptive communication pattern is *overgeneralization*. It refers to the tendency to draw global conclusions in response to isolated events. Here's how it would sound from a parent:

MOTHER: Ernesto, can you please explain to me why you never do your homework?

ERNESTO: What are you talking about? I do my homework every night!

MOTHER: Your teachers told me you have a few missing assignments this semester.

ERNESTO: So does everybody! What's the big deal? I miss a few assignments, and you're ready to call in the damn cavalry!

MOTHER: Why do you always give me such a hard time? I just want what's best for you.

ERNESTO: Stay out of my damn business! That's what's best for me!

What a shame, because there may actually be ways in which Ernesto's mother could help him with his homework or at least get some of the reassurance she was looking for about his completion of homework assignments. Not by starting the discussion with an overgeneralization, though. While other children are sometimes able to bypass their parents' overgeneralizations and get to the real issues, many kids often react strongly to such statements and may lack the skills to respond appropriately with corrective information.

You're best off phrasing things as an unsolved problem ("Ernesto, your teachers tell me you're missing a few homework assignments . . . What's up?") and leaving the overgeneralizations on the shelf.

Another common tendency, *perfectionism*, sometimes prevents parents from acknowledging the progress their child has made and makes them cling to an old, unmodified vision of the child's capabilities. Perfectionism is often driven less by the child's lack of progress and more by the parents' own anxiety. Wherever it's coming from, perfectionism is usually counterproductive when applied to a child who may be tired of receiving feedback on practically everything they do or who may feel enormously frustrated by their parents' unrealistic expectations:

> **FATHER:** Erica, your mother and I are pretty pleased about how much better you're doing in school, but you're still not working as hard as you ought to be.
>
> **ERICA:** Huh?
>
> **MOTHER:** We think you should be working harder.
>
> **ERICA:** I get my work done, don't I?
>
> **FATHER:** Yes, apparently you do, but we want you to do extra math problems over the weekend so you can get even better at it.
>
> **ERICA:** Extra math problems? I already have too much homework over the weekend.
>
> **FATHER:** Well, that may be true, but we really think the extra math will be very helpful to you.

ERICA: I'm not doing extra math problems over the weekend. I need a break over the weekend.

MOTHER: We're just trying to look out for you. Now, your father and I have already talked this over, so there's no discussion on it.

ERICA: No freaking way.

Hmm. Erica may or may not actually be interested in thinking about how to improve in math. Either way, her parents would be far better off approaching her about it through Plan B.

Here are some other maladaptive communication patterns you'll want to avoid:

- **SARCASM:** Sarcastic remarks are often totally lost on kids who are black-and-white thinkers, because they don't have the skills to figure out that the parent means the exact opposite of what they actually said.

- **PUT-DOWNS:** These are not a great way to engage a kid in solving problems collaboratively ("What's the matter with you?! Why can't you be more like your sister?").

- **CATASTROPHIZING:** This is where parents greatly exaggerate the effect of current behavior on a child's future well-being ("We've resigned ourselves to the fact that Jamie will probably end up in jail someday").

- **INTERRUPTING:** Don't forget, the child is probably having trouble sorting through his thoughts in the first place. Your interruptions don't help.

- **LECTURING:** "How many times do I have to tell you . . ." Well, you've probably told them more than enough times, so it's better to switch gears and try to figure out and resolve whatever is getting in the way of your kid doing what you've been telling them to do.

- **DWELLING ON THE PAST:** "Listen, kid, your duck's been upside down in the water for a long time. You think I'm gonna get all excited just because you've put together a few good weeks?" Ouch.

- **TALKING THROUGH A THIRD PERSON:** "You're not going out with your friends this weekend, and your father is going to tell you why. Isn't that right, dear?" Whether you're hiding behind someone else or not, Plan A is not the ideal way to get your concerns addressed.

GRANDPARENTS

At times it's necessary to bring grandparents into the mix on understanding, and perhaps helping, a kid with concerning behaviors. In many families, grandparents or other relatives function as co-parents, taking care of the children while the parents are at work. Even if grandparents don't spend much time with the child—but never miss an opportunity to tell the parents what they would do if they were in charge—they need to be enlightened about the lagging skills and unsolved problems that set the stage for their grandchild's concerning behavior and helped to understand that the way things were done in the "good old days" doesn't solve any problems durably. By the way, I've seen situations in which grandparents played an absolutely indispensable role in helping a kid with concerning behavior, because it was a grandparent who had the best relationship with the kid and was in the best position to begin the process of solving problems collaboratively.

YOU

This is a statement of the obvious, but a child with concerning behaviors can put tremendous pressure on your mental health and on your marriage. In many two-parent families, one parent is primarily disposed toward imposition of adult will (convinced that more authority would get things squared away), and the other is primarily disposed toward just letting things go (having become convinced that more authority is only making things worse and that family peace is more important than compliance). Since neither approach is working, they have little to show for their predispositions. Yet it's not unusual for the two adults to blame each other for the failure to make much headway on reducing concerning behaviors:

> **PARENT #1:** If you'd just let me deal with her and stop letting her off the hook, things would be different around here!
>
> **PARENT #2:** I'm not going to stand by and watch you screaming at her and punishing her all the time. Somebody needs to give the kid a break!

While it's true that kids with concerning behaviors can cause significant tension between caregivers, it's also true that significant tension between caregivers can make life with a child with concerning behaviors much more difficult. Some partners aren't even very good at collaboratively solving problems with each other, so working on unsolved problems with a child can represent a radically different skill set. Partners who are drained by their own difficulties often have little energy left for a labor-intensive child. Sometimes one partner feels exhausted and resentful that they have to be the primary parent because the other parent spends a lot of time at work.

It's hard to work on helping your child if you're feeling the need to put your own house in order first. Perhaps you've come to recognize that you're lacking some of the same skills as your child with concerning behaviors (this may have become apparent as you were perusing the lagging skills on the ALSUP). Plan B can help you learn new skills right along with your child. Perhaps your child's concerning behaviors are evoking strong emotions in you because those behaviors are reminiscent of traumatic experiences you've endured previously. Plan B can help you reduce those behaviors and feel OK about pursuing expectations and solving problems with your child in a way that is a departure from those abusive experiences. Perhaps you're so drained by work and schedules and the needs of your other children that you simply have very little energy and patience left for the rigors of helping your child with concerning behaviors. Plan B can help you get your energy back. Solved problems aren't energy-drainers, only unsolved problems are. Maybe you're quite bitter about having been dealt a difficult hand. Maybe you'll feel less bitter if your hand improves. Finally, perhaps you feel that you need to get a better handle on your own emotions so you can help your child do the same. You should find the proactive and collaborative aspects of Plan B to be very helpful.

Make sure you take care of yourself. Work hard at finding or creating a support system for yourself. Seek professional help or other forms of support if you need it. These things don't change on their own.

Q & A

QUESTION: My spouse won't use Plan B. They won't even read this book. Any advice?

ANSWER: Your spouse may not have strong beliefs guiding their use of Plan A, it's just what they were raised with, or it's what a lot of books and talk-show hosts and nanny programs tell them to do, and they've never given the matter much thought. The goal, of course, is to help them give the matter some thought, beginning with new information about a child's lagging skills and unsolved problems. Ultimately, the goal is to help them come to the recognition that the child and family will be helped far more if adults view themselves as problem solvers rather than as the swift and unrelenting purveyors of adult-imposed consequences.

For some adults, books aren't the best way to access new information. Maybe your spouse will listen to a CD in the car? Or access information on a website? You'll want to check out www.livesinthebalance.org for lots of potential resources.

There are also many adults who use Plan A because they fear that their concerns won't be heard or addressed if they use any other approach. When did they come to fear that their concerns wouldn't be heard or addressed? Probably during childhood, when their Plan A parents were neither hearing nor addressing their concerns. These adults need to be reassured that their concerns will be heard and addressed using Plan B as well.

QUESTION: But my husband says Plan A worked for him.
ANSWER: It depends what he means by *worked*. While it's true that you can get away with Plan A with a kid

who has the skills to adaptively handle imposition of adult will, I don't think it's healthy under any circumstances for kids' concerns to be dismissed or disregarded, whether you can get away with it or not. The fact that Plan A is causing challenging episodes and hostility and misery suggests that clearly it's not "working" for your child with concerning behaviors.

QUESTION: I've been taught that it's important for parents to be consistent with each other in front of the child so the child can't do any "splitting." So, what advice do you give parents if one is using Plan A on an issue and the other disagrees?

ANSWER: That's worth thinking about a little. Consistency is a bit overrated. I've come across no co-parents who were perfectly consistent with each other. And, by and large, their offspring were well-behaved! Parents do need to agree on the expectations their child is having difficulty meeting and do need to agree on the ones that are a high priority. Then they need to agree on how to go about solving those problems. Problems that are solved with Plan A generally aren't durably solved. It doesn't matter that one parent can "get away" with Plan A if the other can't.

QUESTION: My other children are not especially challenging and respond well to Plan A. Am I supposed to have two different types of discipline going on in my household at the same time?

ANSWER: Kids who respond to Plan A respond to Plan B as well, so if you're determined to be consistent, use Plan B with your not-so-challenging kids, too. While your not-so-challenging kids might not react as strongly to Plan A as your kid with concerning behaviors, why would you want to deprive the not-so-challenging kids of the benefits of being involved in the process of solving the problems that affect their lives?

• • •

Sandra had her first meeting with the social worker, Ms. Brennan, on the inpatient unit after work the next day.

"That lip looks pretty bad," said Ms. Brennan.

"It looks worse than it feels," said Sandra, lying.

"From what I can gather, you and Frankie have been down this route before," said Ms. Brennan.

"You mean him hitting me or him being on an inpatient unit?"

"Well, both, I guess."

"I've been hit many times," said Sandra. "Not usually this bad. He's always sorry afterward. We don't really interact with each other much anymore, so I haven't been getting hit lately. And, yeah, he's been hospitalized a few times before this. It's never really accomplished much. To tell you the truth, I think the other inpatient units did more harm than good."

"I'm sorry to hear that," said Ms. Brennan. "I thought I'd talk with you for a few minutes before we bring Frankie in on the discussion. From what I can gather, it's been a long haul for you and Frankie."

"I think Frankie's had a hard life. I was sixteen years old when I had him. We lived in a homeless shelter when he was younger. But we did OK back then. Now, like I said, we don't really communicate much anymore. And when we do, it's ugly."

"I understand," said Ms. Brennan.

No, you don't, thought Sandra. "All I know is I've done my best. I mean, that kid is my life. I just don't know what to do."

"You seem to be blaming yourself for Frankie's difficulties."

"Well, who the hell else is there to blame?" Sandra asked. "The school blames me, the therapists blame me, his case worker blames me. I'm elected." Sandra was a little surprised at how angry she was.

"We don't blame people around here," said Ms. Brennan. "We assume parents do the best they can."

Sandra pondered this. "Well, my best clearly wasn't good enough."

"We see a lot of that around here," said Ms. Brennan.

"A lot of what?"

"A lot of parents who've tried really hard but don't have much to show for it."

"This lip is what I have to show for it," said Sandra.

"I think that kids like Frankie require a pretty specialized approach," said Ms. Brennan, "and that a lot of what seems to work for most kids doesn't work for kids like Frankie."

"Nothing against you, but we've had a lot of people try to help us. And I'm still getting hit. So, I'm kind of skeptical."

"I don't blame you. But I think one thing is obvious. We really need to help you and Frankie start talking to each other, but in a way that doesn't cause you to get hit."

"That would be good. I just . . . I don't know if it's very likely."

"Well, I'd like to hear a little about what it is that you still try talking with him about, and how you try to do it. Then I might help you do it a different way. What do you try to talk to him about?"

"School mostly," said Sandra. "I mean, we live in a pretty small apartment, so there's all the crap that goes along with living in a tight space. How loud he plays his music, how much time he spends playing video games, what video games he's playing, putting his dirty clothes in the laundry basket. But it's mostly school. I'm really worried that he's going to get thrown out of the program he's in, and I don't know what we're going to do if that happens."

"How do you try talking with him about those things?"

"Well, I mostly try not talking with him about those things," said Sandra, "because I don't want it to get ugly. But the more I think about it, the more worried I get, and then I can't help but talk to him about it, but by then I'm so stressed out about it that I'm probably not very calm when I do it, and then it goes downhill pretty fast."

"If I was to ask Frankie about why you and he don't talk anymore, what do you think he'd say?" asked Ms. Brennan.

"He'd say I don't listen," said Sandra. "He says that all the time. Maybe he's right."

"We're going to find out," said Ms. Brennan. "But I'd like to teach you a way to solve those problems with him—school, the loud music, the laundry, the video games—that I'm pretty sure won't cause him to feel that you're not listening to him. We're going to need lots of information from Frankie for those problems to get solved. Once they're solved—and once you and Frankie are able to solve problems together—I don't think you're going to get hit anymore."

Ms. Brennan explained Plan B and the three steps of Plan B. "So, what I'd like to do is try talking with Frankie about a problem, and I think the fact that he hates his program at school is a good place to start. Not that it's the only thing that we need to talk with him about, but it sounds like it's the primary source of conflict for you two. All I'm going to do right now is the Empathy step. You can join in if you'd like, but the main thing is for you to see what the information-gathering process looks like. We really want to understand what's hard for him about school."

"OK," said Sandra.

Frankie shuffled in with a staff member. He meekly said hi to Sandra.

"Hi, Frankie," said Sandra. "Do you have everything you need here?"

Frankie nodded. "I'm sorry I hit you."

"I know."

"I just needed you to stop talking," said Frankie.

"I think," said Ms. Brennan, "that I might be able to help you and your mom talk together in a way that works better."

"I don't like talking to my mom."

"How come?" asked Ms. Brennan.

"She's like . . . she gets too flipped out about everything."

"Like what?"

Frankie sighed. "She's always stressed about money, and work . . . and me. It's just easier if we just don't talk."

"From what I can gather, there are a lot of things that you should probably be talking about," said Ms. Brennan.

"Yeah, but not to her."

"To whom?"

"I don't know," said Frankie. "Not her."

"So, I heard you say that she's too stressed out about every-thing. How does that make it hard for you to talk to her?"

"She doesn't listen," said Frankie. "She just kinda barges in my room and goes totally ape on me. It's not talking . . . it's just, like, she's crazed."

"Shall we see if your mom can listen now while I talk to you about school?" asked Ms. Brennan.

"I don't really see the point," said Frankie. He looked at Sandra. "You're the one who let them put me in that freaking program. You didn't even freaking ask me."

Sandra wasn't sure what to say. She looked to Ms. Brennan for help. "Go ahead," Ms. Brennan encouraged.

"Frankie, I agreed for you to be in that program because the people at school said it was the best thing for you. I guess it was the wrong decision. But I didn't know what else to do. I've never known what to do." Sandra started tearing up.

Frankie looked at Ms. Brennan. "I'm not doing this."

"How come?" Ms. Brennan asked.

"She's already crying. I don't wanna have to deal with that crap. That's why I like talking to the staff here. They listen, they don't freak out."

Sandra covered her face.

"See what I mean!" said Frankie, jumping out of his chair. "I don't want to do this!"

"You don't have to do it," said Ms. Brennan. "But hear me out for a second. Then you can decide if you want to stay."

Frankie stood by the door of Ms. Brennan's office.

"I could be wrong, but I have a feeling your mother is tougher than you think. Her life hasn't been easy."

"I know her life hasn't been easy! I thought we were talking about my life!"

"Let's do that," said Ms. Brennan. "All I'm saying is that I think your mom can listen to what you have to say."

"Without crying? Or yelling?"

"I can't promise you that she won't cry. I don't think she's going to yell, because you'll be talking to me. Your mom is just going to listen."

Frankie was silent.

"Can you talk to me about the things you don't like about your school?" asked Ms. Brennan.

"Yes."

"Can your mom stay in the room while we're talking?"

"If she keeps crying, I'm leaving," said Frankie.

"That's fine," said Ms. Brennan. She turned to Sandra. "Can you listen to what Frankie has to say about his school without crying?"

"I'll try," said Sandra.

Frankie sat back down.

"So, tell me about the difficulties you've been having at school. What's going on with that?"

"I want to go back to my regular junior high school," said Frankie, glancing warily at Sandra.

"That's good to know," said Ms. Brennan, immediately recognizing that Frankie had voiced a solution rather than a concern. She steered the discussion back to Frankie's concerns. "I hear that's what you want to do, but I don't understand what it is that's making you want to do that."

"The kids in my program are freaks. And the teachers are losers. And I don't want to be a 'speddie' anymore," said Frankie, using the colloquial term for a child receiving special education services. "I wanna be normal."

"That's a lot of reasons," said Ms. Brennan.

"And I don't want my mom making decisions about me without me." Frankie glanced at Sandra again.

"OK," said Ms. Brennan. "Is there anything else you want to say about any of those things?"

"Not really," said Frankie.

"What do you mean that you don't want to be a 'speddie' anymore?" asked Ms. Brennan.

"I've been getting into trouble at school for a long time," said Frankie. "It's not like I'm trying to get into trouble. But no one's ever helped me not get in trouble. All that happens is they give me detentions, or they suspend me, and then my mom gets pissed at me at home. It's, like, pointless to even go to school. And now I'm stuck with a bunch of freaks who are way more messed up than I am."

"So, you feel it's the wrong program for you," said Ms. Brennan.

"At least I had friends at my old school," said Frankie. "Even if I was getting into trouble, at least I had friends."

"It's helpful for us to hear this," said Ms. Brennan. "And your mom seems to be hanging in there."

"That's 'cuz you're here," said Frankie.

"Maybe so," said Ms. Brennan. "But I think I can help you

talk to each other without me. We'll be practicing while you're here. This conversation is the first step. Frankie, you have a lot to say, and I hope you'll keep giving your mom the chance to listen. Because I know she's going to try very hard to get better at hearing your concerns. These problems that are causing you to fight with each other . . . well, it's going to take both of you, working together, to solve them."

11

UNSOLVED PROBLEMS AT SCHOOL

As hard as it is to help a kid with concerning behaviors within a family, it may be even harder in a school. After all, there are twenty or thirty other students in the child's classes, with a wide range of special needs. Like parents, most general education teachers and school administrators haven't received any specialized training to help them understand and help kids with concerning behaviors, and those who have received training probably learned more about Plan A than Plan B. There are a lot of different people to get on the same page. And there's a big dinosaur in the building: the existing school discipline program.

Fortunately, many kids who exhibit concerning behaviors at home don't exhibit concerning behaviors at school. This pattern often reinforces the false belief that kids' concerning behaviors are completely under their control. Of course, if you read the first few chapters of this book, you know that that belief comes from obsolete lenses. Here are a few alternative explanations for the home–school disparity:

- **THE SITUATIONAL FACTOR**: As you've read, concerning behaviors occur when a kid is having difficulty meeting certain expectations. The expectations at home and school are often quite different. For example, because the school environment tends to be relatively structured and predictable, it can actually be more "user-friendly" for some kids than the home environment.

- **THE EMBARRASSMENT FACTOR**: Many kids with concerning behaviors would be absolutely mortified if their classmates and teachers witnessed those behaviors, so they put massive amounts of energy into holding it together at school. But since the potential for embarrassment decreases at home, and since the energy can't be maintained 24/7, the kids unravel the minute they get home. Most of us are better behaved outside the home than we are inside, so kids with concerning behaviors aren't especially unusual in this regard. Of course, there are kids whose frustration at school blows right through the embarrassment factor.

- **THE CHEMICAL FACTOR:** Teachers and classmates are often the primary beneficiaries of pharmacotherapy because kids with concerning behaviors may be medicated during school hours, but many medications wear off by late afternoon or early evening, just in time for the child to decompensate at home.

The fact that concerning behaviors aren't occurring at school doesn't mean that school isn't contributing to concerning behaviors that occur elsewhere. Many things can happen at school to fuel episodes outside of school: being teased by other kids, feeling socially isolated or rejected, feeling frustrated and embarrassed over struggles on certain academic tasks, feeling misunderstood by the teacher. Homework, of course, often extends academic frustrations well beyond the end of the school day. So, schools still have a role to play in helping kids with concerning behaviors, even if they don't see the kid at his worst.

This chapter is primarily focused on the kids who do have challenging episodes at school. Luckily, everything you've read in this book so far is as applicable to schools and classrooms as it is to homes and families. But implementation at school isn't easy. Many (if not most) school discipline programs have a strong orientation toward Plan A; intervention for students with concerning behaviors occurs, all too often, in the heat of the moment rather than proactively; evaluations of teachers and schools are based primarily on the performance of their students on high-stakes tests, with precious little emphasis on the social, emotional, and behavioral gains of the most vulnerable students; budgets are extremely tight; time is short. In many instances teachers justifiably feel that they lack the expertise and are not being provided with the kind of support they need to understand and help kids with concerning behaviors. While educators deal with lagging *academic* skills all the time, they are often unfamiliar with the lagging skills that make it difficult for a student to respond adaptively to problems and frustrations. This is especially interesting in view of the fact that the majority of concerning behaviors that occur at school can be linked to difficulties students are having with academics.

And to make things still worse, misguided, ineffective zero-tolerance policies have driven many schools to use discipline rubric systems, which are usually comprised of a list (often a long one) of behaviors students shouldn't exhibit and an algorithm of adult-imposed consequences attached to each behavior on the list. The research that has accumulated over the years is crystal clear on several points: zero-tolerance policies have made things worse, not better; standard school disciplinary practices generally aren't effective for the students to whom they are most frequently applied and aren't needed for the students to whom they are never applied. The school discipline program isn't the reason well-behaved students behave well. They behave well *because they can*. We have little good to show for the millions of punishments—detentions, suspensions, expulsions—that are meted out every year to the kids who are having difficulty handling the social, emotional, and behavioral expectations at school. And yet most administrators' standard rationale for the continued use of consequences goes something like this:

> We have to set an example for all of our students; even if suspension doesn't help Frankie, at least it sets an example for our other students. We need to let them know that we take this kind of behavior seriously at our school.

QUESTION: What message do we give the other students if we continue to apply interventions that aren't helping Frankie behave more adaptively?
ANSWER: That we're actually not sure how to help our students with concerning behaviors.

QUESTION: What's the likelihood that the students who don't exhibit concerning behaviors will begin to exhibit concerning behaviors if we did not make an example of Frankie?
ANSWER: As a general rule, slim to none.

QUESTION: What message do we give Frankie if we continue to apply strategies that aren't working?
ANSWER: We don't understand you and we can't help you.

QUESTION: Under which circumstance do we have the best chance of helping Frankie solve the problems that are setting in motion his concerning behaviors: when he's in school, or when he's suspended from school?
ANSWER: When he's in school.

QUESTION: Why do many schools continue to use interventions that aren't working for their students with concerning behaviors?
ANSWER: They aren't sure what else to do.

QUESTION: What happens to students to whom these interventions are counterproductively applied for many years?
ANSWER: They become more disenfranchised and alienated and fall farther outside the social fabric of the school.

QUESTION: Isn't it the parents' job to make their child behave at school?
ANSWER: Helping a child deal more adaptively with frustration is everyone's job. Also, we can't escape the fact that the parents aren't there when the child is having difficulty meeting expectations at school.

QUESTION: Isn't it the job of special education to handle these children?

ANSWER: Actually, special education often has very little to offer many such students.

QUESTION: What usually happens to students with concerning behaviors when we apply a sink-or-swim mentality?

ANSWER: They sink.

Time for Plan B. But solving problems collaboratively in a school is no small undertaking. Here are some of the necessary components:

- **AWARENESS:** Students with concerning behaviors are being ill-served by traditional disciplinary practices in many schools. Some educators know this already and are eager to learn new ways of understanding and helping these kids. Other educators still don't know this and need to be enlightened.

- **URGENCY:** Understanding and helping these students has to be a priority. However, since educators have so many different competing priorities, helping students with concerning behaviors often sits quite low on the list. But we're losing a lot of kids unnecessarily because their concerning behaviors are misunderstood and mishandled.

- **EXPERTISE:** Many schools have been using the same discipline strategies for decades, even though it's quite clear that the "frequent fliers"—the students who are chronically in the office, in detention, being suspended, being paddled, and/or being restrained and secluded—aren't benefiting from those strategies. Equally clear is the fact that those strategies don't address the true difficulties (lagging skills and unsolved problems) of students with concerning behaviors. Some educators believe that the expertise necessary for understanding and helping behaviorally challenging students is well beyond their grasp. Not true. The expertise required is the same for everyone: identifying lagging skills and unsolved problems and using Plan B.

- **MENTALITY:** It's time to stop blaming parents for concerning behaviors that occur at school. Blaming parents is a distracting, counterproductive dead end, and it makes it much harder for school staff to focus on the problems they could be busy solving. Parents of kids with concerning behaviors get much more blame than they deserve for their kids' difficulties, in the same way that parents of well-behaved kids get much more credit than they deserve for their kids' positive attributes. While it is true that there are many students who come from home situations that might not be considered "ideal," it is also true that most of those students are well-behaved.

- **TIME:** Classroom teachers often feel that they don't have time to help kids with concerning behaviors and that it is more efficient to simply let folks in the office handle things. The problem, of course, is that the folks in the office don't really know much about the unsolved problems that are causing the behaviors that are prompting teachers to send kids to the office. So, the folks in the office have little to offer when it comes to solving problems with students. The folks in the office may have a great deal to offer when it comes to providing coverage for classroom teachers who have problems to solve with their students. While Plan B does take time, it also saves time. Time is almost always a major concern *before* teachers and administrators learn how to use Plan B, but those concerns fade once educators make it a priority to understand and help these kids and become skilled at Plan B. When do staff members in these schools do Plan B? Sometimes before school, sometimes after school, sometimes during lunch, sometimes during recess, sometimes during the teacher's prep time. I've yet to meet the administrator who isn't willing to arrange for coverage so that a classroom teacher can use Proactive Plan B with an individual student. Some schools have found it worthwhile to retool the entire schedule to create the time needed for helping kids who would otherwise become lost in the shuffle.

- **ASSESSMENT AND REFERRAL MECHANISMS:** It will be necessary to achieve a consensus on the lagging skills and unsolved problems of each student with concerning behaviors so that the factors underlying their difficulties are well understood and the problems that need to be solved are clear. The ALSUP should be the standard pre-referral, triage instrument in every school. The information provided by the ALSUP should provide the foundation for writing functional behavior assessments (FBAs), individualized education plans (IEPs), and behavior plans. It's crucial to go further than simply concluding that a student's concerning behaviors are *working* at getting them something they want (for example, attention) and escaping and avoiding tasks and situations that are difficult, uncomfortable, tedious, or scary. A good functional assessment needs to explain why a student is going about getting, escaping, and avoiding in such a maladaptive fashion (lagging skills) and when that is occurring (unsolved problems).

- **PRACTICE, FEEDBACK, AND COACHING:** Once mechanisms for assessing lagging skills and unsolved problems are in place, schools are ready for the next step: becoming proficient at Plan B. For most people, this is a process that will require practice and ongoing feedback and coaching. This can take a variety of forms in different schools, and a variety of resources are available for support (details, once again, at

www.livesinthebalance.org). The aspects of Plan B that
are challenging for parents tend to be the same for
educators: drilling for information in the Empathy step;
articulating why it's important that an expectation be
met in the Define Adult Concerns step; collaborating
on solutions that are realistic and mutually satisfactory.

- **ONGOING COMMUNICATION:** Because Proactive Plan B is
far preferable to Emergency Plan B, advance prepara-
tion and good communication among adults are essential. The only models for treatment that don't require
good communication are the ineffective ones. To help
out, another instrument, the Problem-Solving Plan, can
be found at www.livesinthebalance.org as well. It was
designed to help adults keep track of the high-priority
unsolved problems that are currently being addressed
with an individual student, to specify who's taking
primary responsibility for solving each problem with
the student, and to track the progression of problem-
solving efforts through the steps of Plan B.

  In schools (as well as in homes) there's a tendency
to work on the "hot" problem that precipitated a concerning behavior on a particular day. But since unsolved problems wax and wane, the "hot" unsolved
problem that was addressed one day or week (but not
seen through to a final resolution) is often replaced
the next day or week by a different "hot" unsolved
problem. However, the first unsolved problem hasn't
gone away; it's just gone into "hibernation." Since it's

still unsolved, it keeps coming back. The Problem-Solving Plan is designed to prevent that from happening by helping adults track unsolved problems over time until they're durably solved. The need for ongoing monitoring means that the adults who are working with a given child will have to reconvene periodically to assess progress and revisit unsolved problems.

- **PERSEVERANCE:** There is no quick fix. You're in this for the long haul. Transforming school discipline is a project. It doesn't happen overnight. But it needs to happen.

Naturally, there's much more that could be said about each of these components. That's why I wrote *Lost at School*, which was published in 2008 and revised in 2020.

This might be a good time to point out that Plan B isn't limited to adult–child problem solving. The ingredients of Plan B are equally applicable to unsolved problems between two kids as well as to those that affect an entire group of kids. And Plan B has significant ramifications for adult–adult problem solving as well. For the remainder of this chapter, let's see what Plan B would look like as applied to these different types of problem solving in a school setting. We'll start with Plan B involving a teacher and student, move on to Plan B between groups of students, and finish with parents and teachers.

STUDENT–TEACHER PROBLEM SOLVING

As you'll see, Proactive Plan B doesn't look much different when the adult is a teacher rather than a parent. The ingredients are exactly the same though the topics may differ. Here's an example between a teacher and a thirteen-year-old:

> **TEACHER:** Class, please get to work on your social studies projects.
>
> **RICKEY:** I'm not doing it.
>
> **TEACHER:** Well, then your grade will reflect both your attitude and your lack of effort.
>
> **RICKEY:** I don't give a damn about my grades. I can't do this crap.
>
> **TEACHER:** Your mouth just bought you a detention, young man. And I don't want students in my classroom who don't do their work. Anything else you'd like to say?
>
> **RICKEY:** Yeah, this class sucks.
>
> **TEACHER:** Nor do I need to listen to this. You need to go to the assistant principal's office NOW.

Oops. That was Plan A, wasn't it? Tricky author. Let's consider our other options. Since this problem was being handled emergently, that would be Emergency Plan C or Emergency Plan B. Here's what Emergency Plan C would look like:

> **TEACHER:** Class, please get to work on your social studies projects.
> **RICKEY:** I'm not doing it.
> **TEACHER:** You're not doing it.
> **RICKEY:** Forget it. I can't do this! Just leave me alone! Damn!
> **TEACHER:** Rickey, you don't have to do it. But hang on for just a second . . . let me get everyone else going, and then you and I can figure out what's the matter and see what we can do about it.

And here's what the same problem would look like if it were handled with Emergency Plan B:

> **TEACHER:** Class, please get to work on your social studies projects.
> **RICKEY:** I'm not doing it.
> **TEACHER:** Tell me what's going on, bud.
> **RICKEY:** Forget it. I can't do this! Just leave me alone! Damn!
> **TEACHER:** Rickey, tell me what's going on.
> **RICKEY:** You know I have trouble with the spelling!
> **TEACHER:** Yes, I do know that. That's why I don't grade you for the spelling.

RICKEY: But it still bugs me!

TEACHER: Let's see if we can find a way for you to do the important part of the assignment—letting me know what you thought of the story you just heard, which is something you're very good at—without you getting frustrated about the spelling part.

RICKEY: How?

TEACHER: Well, maybe Darren would help you with any words you don't know how to spell.

RICKEY: No way.

TEACHER: How come?

RICKEY: He's going to rag on me about needing his help.

TEACHER: Hmm. Is there anyone who could help you who wouldn't give you a hard time about it?

RICKEY: DeJuan.

TEACHER: DeJuan? That could work. You'd feel more comfortable with him?

RICKEY: Yeah, he's smart.

TEACHER: You're smart, too. You just have some trouble with spelling.

Of course, it would be far better to handle this problem proactively, especially since this isn't the first time it's occurred. In other words, Rickey's spelling problem is predictable. So rather than dealing with the spelling problem emergently, every day, which is very time-consuming, the teacher would want to schedule a time to solve the problem with Rickey using Proactive Plan B, preferably before it erupts again in the middle of another lesson.

By the way, the ingredients of Plan B can be applied to every student in the class, each of whom has problems that need to be solved. If every student is working on something, then the student with concerning behaviors doesn't stick out like a sore thumb.

STUDENT–STUDENT AND GROUP PROBLEM SOLVING

Plan B can also be applied to unsolved problems that may arise between two students. In such instances, the teacher's role is Plan B facilitator. Here's an example from *Lost at School*:

MR. BARTLETT: Hank, as you know, in our classroom when something is bothering somebody we try to talk about it. As I mentioned to you yesterday, I thought it might be a good idea for me and you and Laura to talk together about the project you guys are supposed to be doing together.

HANK: OK.

MR. BARTLETT: She has some concerns about what it's going to be like doing the project with you. It sounds like you guys worked on a project together last year, yes?

HANK: Yup.

MR. BARTLETT: I don't know if you knew this, but Laura

came away from that project feeling like you weren't very receptive to her ideas and feeling like she did most of the work. So, she wasn't too sure she wanted to do this project with you.

HANK: She doesn't have to do the project with me. I can find another partner.

MR. BARTLETT: Yes, she was thinking the same thing. But I was hoping we could find a way for you guys to work well together. What do you think of Laura's concern?

HANK: I don't know. That was a long time ago.

MR. BARTLETT: Do you remember how you guys figured out what to do on last year's project?

HANK: No.

MR. BARTLETT: Do you remember Laura doing most of the work?

HANK: Sort of. But that's because she didn't like the way I was doing it, so she decided to do it herself.

LAURA: That is so not true. I did most of the work because you wouldn't do anything. And you wouldn't listen to any of my ideas.

HANK: Well, that's not how I remember it.

MR. BARTLETT: It sounds like you both have different recollections about what happened last year and why it didn't go so well, so maybe we shouldn't concentrate so much on what happened last year. I don't know if you would ever agree on that. Maybe we should focus on the concerns that are getting in the way of your working together this year. Laura, your concern is that Hank won't listen to any of your ideas. And you're both concerned about the possibility that Laura will do all the work. I wonder if there's a way for you guys to make sure that you have equal input into the design of the project, without having Laura do all the work in the end. Do you guys have any ideas?

LAURA: This is so pointless. He won't listen to my ideas.

MR. BARTLETT: Well, I know that's what you feel happened last year, but I can't do anything about last year. We're trying to focus on this year and on coming up with a solution so that you and Hank have equal input and work equally hard.

LAURA: Can you sit with us while we're figuring out what to do? Then you'll see what I mean.

HANK: Then you'll see what I mean.

MR. BARTLETT: So, Laura, you're saying that maybe if I sit in on your discussions, I might be able to help you guys have a more equal exchange of ideas?

LAURA: That's not really what I meant.

MR. BARTLETT: I know, but I'm thinking that it might not be a bad way to ensure the equal exchange of ideas. What do you think?

HANK: I think we can work together.

LAURA: Fine, sit in on our discussion and help us have equal input.

MR. BARTLETT: Only if that works for you guys.

LAURA: It only works for me if I have to work with him.

MR. BARTLETT: I'm not saying you have to work with him. I'm saying I'd like you to give it a shot so the other kids don't have to break up their pairs. We can entertain other options if that solution doesn't work for you.

LAURA: What other solutions?

MR. BARTLETT: I don't know. Whatever we come up with. Can you guys think of any others?

HANK: We could do the project by ourselves, you know, alone. She could do one and I could do one.

MR. BARTLETT: Well, that would probably work for you guys, but it wouldn't work for me. One of the goals of this project was for kids to learn to work together. I think it's an important skill.

LAURA: Why don't we try to work together, with you helping us, and if that doesn't work we can do our own projects.

MR. BARTLETT: Hank, does that solution work for you?

HANK: Sure, whatever.

MR. BARTLETT: I need to think about whether it works for me. You guys'll try hard to work together with me helping you?

LAURA: Yes.

HANK: Yes.

MR. BARTLETT: OK, let's go with it. We're working on the project again tomorrow. I'll sit in on your discussion with each other and see if I can help make sure the exchange of ideas is equal and the workload is equal. Let's see how it goes.

While some problems are best addressed by using Plan B with individual students or pairs of students, other problems, especially those that affect the group as a whole, are best addressed by using Plan B with the entire classroom community. Group discussions are a common occurrence in many classrooms, but mostly on topics that have an academic orientation. But when the three steps of Plan B are added to a group discussion, and when such discussions are about nonacademic problems such as bullying, teasing, and general classroom conduct, then community members learn to listen to and take into account one another's concerns and recognize that there are no "right" answers, only solutions that are mutually satisfactory. Group problem solving is hard, but no harder and messier than having problems that never get solved or having problems that "go underground" because there is no mechanism for solving them.

Yet again, the ingredients are the same, and the classroom teacher is the facilitator. The first goal is to achieve the clearest possible understanding of the concerns of each group member with regard to a given problem. Once the concerns have been well clarified, the group moves on to the next challenge: finding a solution that will address those concerns. The criteria for a good solution remain the same: it must be realistic and mutually satisfactory.

When using Plan B with a group, the teacher helps the group decide what problems to tackle first, keeps the group focused and serious (group members will eventually take on these responsibilities as well), and ensures that the exploration of concerns and solutions is exhaustive. The teacher's stance in helping the group sort through concerns and solutions is generally neutral. There are no good or bad concerns, no such thing as "competing" concerns, only concerns that need to be addressed. Likewise, there are no right or wrong solutions, only ones that are realistic (or not) and mutually satisfactory (or not). There's an excellent video of full-class Plan B on the Lives in the Balance website.

PARENT–TEACHER PROBLEM SOLVING

Parents of kids with concerning behaviors and school personnel often have difficulty working together for the same reasons that kids and adults do: the tendency to blame one party or another; the failure to achieve a consensus on the true nature of a kid's difficulties (lagging skills) and the true events (unsolved problems) precipitating his explosions; the failure to identify the concerns of the respective parties; and the attempt of one party to impose its will on another. As Sara Lawrence-Lightfoot writes in her insightful book *The Essential Conversation: What Parents and Teachers Can Learn from Each Other*, great potential exists for productive collaboration between parents and teachers. When parents and teachers are able to exchange highly specific information about a child's lagging skills and unsolved problems, they start trusting each other. Parents become convinced that they are being heard and that the teacher sees, knows, and cares about their child. Educators become convinced that the parents are eager for information, eager to collaborate, and eager to help in any way possible. Both parties need to be part of the process of working toward a mutually satisfactory action plan. You're on the same team.

Here's what Proactive Plan B looks like between parents and teachers. Once again, it uses the same ingredients: information gathering and understanding, entering the concerns of both parties into consideration, and brainstorming solutions that are realistic and mutually satisfactory.

TEACHER: I understand that homework has been very difficult lately.

MOTHER: Homework has been very difficult for a very long time. You're the first teacher Rickey's had who's expressed any interest in what we go through with homework. We spend several hours fighting over homework every weeknight and every weekend.

TEACHER: I'm sorry about that. But let's see if we can figure out what's so hard about homework and then come up with a plan so it's not so terrible anymore.

MOTHER: You can't imagine how nice that would be.

TEACHER: Can you tell me the parts of homework that have been difficult for you and Rickey? Or is it all hard? You don't mind if I write these down, do you?

MOTHER: Not at all. He's a very slow writer. So, he gets frustrated that homework takes as long as it does. And he seems to have trouble thinking of a lot of the details you're asking for. And he's always struggled with spelling. Last year's teacher told us not to worry about the spelling. But Rickey doesn't seem to be able to do that. So, I don't know whether to forget about it or work on it. I wouldn't know how to work on it anyway! And I end up doing a lot of the writing for him.

TEACHER: Yes, I've noticed the slow writing part, and the difficulty he has coming up with details, and his troubles with spelling. How about math?

MOTHER: He breezes right through it. Very little writing, very little spelling, and not the kind of details he has trouble with.

TEACHER: Well, then, let's take our problems one at a time. Of course, I've only had Rickey in my class for about four weeks now, so I can't say I have a perfect handle on his difficulties or what we should do about them. And I have begun working with Rickey on these problems myself, so I'm in the midst of trying to gather some information from him, too. But I'm not one for having kids spend two hours on homework every night, and I'm certainly not one for having homework cause problems between kids and their parents. Of course, I'm not always aware that those problems exist, so I appreciate your honesty.

MOTHER: I'm not shy about letting people know what's going on with Rickey. I just wish we were seeing more progress on the problems he's having.

TEACHER: The thing is, we're going to need to get

Rickey involved in the homework discussion, too. Even if you and I come up with brilliant solutions, they won't be so brilliant if he's not on board with them. So maybe we should use this discussion to make sure we have a clear sense of the problems we need to get solved. One problem is the amount of time homework is consuming. Yes?

MOTHER: Yes!

TEACHER: But it sounds like a lot of that time is spent being frustrated over what to work on and how you can help, so that's something we'll need to get solved, too.

MOTHER: Absolutely.

TEACHER: I'm not convinced that Rickey can't get better at spelling, so I'm disinclined to tell you that we should drop it altogether. Plus, as you said, Rickey doesn't seem able to drop it. So spelling is an unsolved problem. And slow writing is an unsolved problem. And fleshing out the details is an unsolved problem. And I know you're doing a lot of the writing for him, but we don't want him getting the idea that he doesn't need to do any of the writing.

MOTHER: Aren't you overwhelmed by all this?

TEACHER: No, I actually find that sorting through unsolved problems helps me be less overwhelmed. At least I know what needs to be addressed.

MOTHER: I see what you mean.

TEACHER: Any other unsolved problems related to homework?

MOTHER: Well, he has hockey practice two nights a

week, so sometimes he's really tired when it's time for homework. Those are our really tough nights.

TEACHER: I can imagine. So, we have some work to do, don't we?

MOTHER: It appears so.

TEACHER: Here's what I'm thinking. If it's OK with you, why don't we meet again within the next week, but next time let's include Rickey in the meeting. Then we can start talking about how these problems can be solved, one at a time.

What's the solution to the writing problem? The spelling problem? The details problem? The hockey practice problem? That's for Rickey, his mom, and his teacher to figure out. There are dozens of possibilities. There's no such thing as a "right" or "wrong" solution—only solutions that are realistic and mutually satisfactory.

Q & A

QUESTION: I'm a teacher, and I'm a little worried about having different sets of expectations for different kids. If I let one kid get away with something, won't my other students try to get away with it as well?

ANSWER: Plan B isn't about letting students get away with something. Teachers have different expectations for different students already. That's what initiatives like differentiated instruction, personalized learning, and universal design are all about (not to mention special education laws).

QUESTION: Does Plan B undermine a teacher's authority with the other kids in the class?

ANSWER: No, it doesn't. The other kids are watching closely. If a teacher intervenes in a way that solves the problems that are causing concerning behaviors, they have done nothing to undermine their authority with the other kids.

QUESTION: Is it really fair to expect teachers—who are not trained as mental health professionals—to solve all these problems with their students?

ANSWER: A mental health degree is not a prerequisite for solving problems collaboratively. Most mental health professionals don't have training in solving problems collaboratively either.

QUESTION: I was using Plan B with a student in my class and things seemed to be going well for a few weeks but then deteriorated again. What happened?

ANSWER: It could be that the solution you and the student agreed on wasn't as realistic and mutually satisfactory as it originally seemed. That's not a sign that you should revert back to Plan A. It's a sign that you need to go back to Plan B to figure out why the solution didn't work as well as anticipated and come up with a revised solution.

QUESTION: Are there some students who are so volatile and unstable that academics should be de-emphasized until things are calmer?

ANSWER: Yes. Some kids simply aren't "available" for academic learning until factors that are impeding their learning—and perhaps stability—have been addressed. Plunging forward with expectations a student clearly can't meet is usually an exercise in futility and often results in detentions, suspensions, expulsions, paddling, restraints, and seclusions.

QUESTION: What if Plan B isn't working? What then?

ANSWER: This is a more interesting question than it might seem, and the answer depends on your definition of the word *working*. For many people, *working* refers only to the ultimate destination, the point at which a problem is finally durably solved. But there are many ways in which Plan B is "working" before the ultimate destination is reached. Plan B is working if adults are viewing a kid's difficulties more accurately and more compassionately. It's working if adults are effectively gathering information about a kid's concerns on a given problem and finally achieving an understanding of what's been getting in the kid's way. It's working if the kid is able to listen to adult concerns and take them into account. Plan B is working if the kid is no longer viewing adults as "the enemy." It's working if the kid is participating in discussions about how a given problem can be solved in a way that addresses the concerns of both parties. Plan B is even working if it's not going so well but the kid and adults haven't broken off discussions and are resolved to keep trying. Yes, the ultimate definition of *working* is that a problem is solved and is no longer causing concerning behaviors. But, sometimes, there are a lot of things that are working before that happens.

QUESTION: But are there some students who need more than what can be provided in a general education setting, even if people are using Plan B?

ANSWER: Yes, there are. But wouldn't it be interesting to see how many students still needed more than what could be provided in general education settings if more general education settings were using Plan B? That question aside, there are some kids who need a larger "dose" of Plan B than can be provided in schools and outpatient settings, kids who continue to behave in an unsafe manner at home, at school, and/or in the community. Many start a downward spiral early, become increasingly alienated, begin exhibiting more serious forms of concerning behavior, and begin to hang out with other children who have come down a similar path. After all else has been tried—therapy, medication, perhaps even alternative day-school placements— what many of these kids ultimately need is a change of environment. A new start. A way to begin working on a new identity. Once alienation and deviance become a kid's identity, things are a lot harder to turn around. Fortunately, there are some outstanding therapeutic day schools and residential facilities in the United States that do an exceptional job of working with such kids.

12

BETTER

You've made it to the last chapter, and you've covered a lot of ground on the way. The first goal was to help you view your child more accurately, beginning with your new lenses: *kids do well if they can.* You now know that it's far more important to focus on your child's unsolved problems than on the concerning behaviors that are being caused by those problems. We dispensed with a lot of the things that are commonly said about concerning behaviors (they're intentional, goal-oriented, and purposeful), about kids who exhibit concerning behaviors (they're unmotivated, attention-seeking, manipulative, coercive, button-pushing), and about the parents of these kids (they're passive, permissive, and inconsistent disciplinarians). You learned why traditional discipline, with its heavy emphasis on rewarding and punishing, may not have improved your situation. We concluded that the sheer force of your will—which may have served you well in other aspects of your life—is not going to be a central ingredient in solving problems with your child. We also decided that you're not going to sacrifice your relationship with your child just because she's having difficulty meeting certain expectations; in fact, your relationship with her is going to play a major role in making things better. We examined the various lagging skills that can make it difficult for your child to respond adaptively to problems and frustrations. We identified the specific expectations your child is having difficulty meeting and prioritized those unsolved problems. You learned how to solve problems, collaboratively and proactively. And you read about the different ways in which Plan B can go awry and how to get things back on track.

My hope is that things are now better in your household. If so, there are a lot of factors that could be at work. Things might be better because you understand your child's difficulties better than you did before. Things might be better because you've removed some low-priority expectations from the equation (Plan C). Maybe things are better because you're relying far less on Plan A and adult-imposed consequences. And things might be better because you and your problem-solving partner have collaboratively and proactively solved a bunch of the problems that were setting in motion concerning behaviors. Along the way, communication has also improved, and you should be feeling like your relationship with your child is moving in the right direction.

Sometimes it's hard to notice that things are getting better. Some adults have a preordained notion of what life is going to be like when things are finally "better" and are disappointed to find that "better" isn't perfect. Your child still has her moments. She's still pretty rigid and inflexible. She can still be irritable or anxious sometimes. Making friends is still hard for her. Some parents wish it weren't so hard to make things better or that it could be accomplished at a faster pace. How hard it is and how quickly progress is achieved differ for every kid and family. And the definition of "better" is different for every kid and family, too. For what it's worth, here's my definition of better: it's better. And better begets better.

If you've been thinking, "Shouldn't all children be raised this way?" the answer is "Yes, of course." You see, while the model described in this book has its roots in the treatment of kids with concerning behaviors, those kids aren't the only ones who could benefit from having their concerns identified and validated, taking another person's concerns into account, participating in the process of generating and considering alternative solutions to problems, working toward mutually satisfactory solutions, and resolving disputes and disagreements without conflict. All kids benefit . . . and so do all adults.

And if you're the type of person who likes to read the entire book before putting what you've read into action, your time has come.

• • •

Sandra and Debbie were on the phone again. It had been a week since Frankie came home from the inpatient unit.

"How's Frankie doing?" asked Debbie.

"Well, he's going to be in the partial hospitalization program in Amberville for a few more weeks," said Sandra. "They're trying to help me get things sorted out with the folks at school, see if there's some way to get Frankie out of that program he hates. I don't know how that's going to pan out, but I feel like people are listening to me—and helping me—instead of just telling me what to do. But the door to his room isn't closed all the time. And he participated in a Plan B conversation yesterday right here in our apartment—about playing his music too loud—with Matt helping out."

"Wow, that's progress," said Debbie.

"Oh, we have a long way to go," said Sandra. "*I* have a long way to go. I didn't know how to talk to my own kid. I didn't know how to solve problems with him. I was trying, but I didn't know how. I was getting so worked up—about how things were going at school especially—that I let it get in the way. I was leaving out the most important person . . . Frankie. I'm seeing him in a very different way now. I think that may be the most important part. I feel like I have a piece of my son back."

"I feel the same way about Jennifer," said Debbie.

"I haven't heard about Jennifer in the past few weeks," said Sandra. "I'm sorry."

"I think you've been a little busy," said Debbie. "Jennifer's talking. More with me than with Kevin, though he's trying hard. It's not easy for him to resist the temptation to rush through the Empathy step and head straight for solutions. But she corrects him when he does it."

"*She* tells *him* how to do Plan B?"

"Yeah, it's actually kind of funny. But we're finding out what's going on in that head of hers. She sure is rigid about some things. But we're getting some problems solved."

"That's wonderful."

"And she's letting me tuck her in to bed at night again. She even let me hug her the other day without getting all pissed off about it."

"No! She did?"

"Well, I gave her advance warning that a hug was coming. She also screamed at me a few minutes later because I'd rearranged something in her room. So, we have a lot more problems to solve." Debbie paused. "Do you think our lives will ever be normal?"

Sandra laughed. "My life hasn't been normal since the day I came into this world. I stopped shooting for normal a long time ago. Abnormal is my normal!"

Debbie pondered this. "So normal isn't even the goal."

"I know it sounds corny, but I'm just concentrating on doing what I can to make tomorrow slightly better than today for me and my kid. That's what I've always done. I don't know what's around the bend. But I'm starting to feel like I know how I'll handle it—whatever it is—when I get there."

"And it's a lot easier when your kid is your partner instead of your enemy."

"Easier, for sure. Easy, no way."

• • •

As you'd imagine, I receive a lot of email from parents and other caregivers. Many ask for help and guidance, others are seeking resources, and quite a few just want to let me know how things are going with their child. The following email, which I received from a father about twelve years ago, was especially memorable:

This evening, after my twelve-year-old daughter stayed up late to finish a project for school, I couldn't help but reflect on how much she has changed in the past twenty months. Today she is a well-balanced student athlete with a great circle of friends. She demonstrates patience and good communication skills. Twenty months ago, she was certainly a behaviorally challenging child. We were quite certain that the only path to resolution was inpatient treatment. While we made some small advances in our understanding of her issues with local psychologists, we made little if any steps toward improvement. Then we read *The Explosive Child*. The issues and solutions became understandable and actionable. Without any professional help we implemented the solutions in the book, and over time the results have been amazing. I am writing to express my gratitude for providing the insights to restore normalcy in our lives. My child is back on the path to a productive and successful life. I have also learned a great deal about myself and human interaction in the process. I consider this the greatest accomplishment of my life.

Kids do well if they can. So do parents. And if things aren't going well for you and your child . . . now you know what to do.

INDEX

drilling (*cont.*)
  primary goal of, 87
  riskiest strategy, 88
  strategies, 87–89
dwelling on the past, 189

Emergency Plan B, 108, 117,
  146, 176, 213
Emergency Plan C, 79
Empathy step (Plan B), 75,
  83–86, 115, 163, 176
  beginning of, 85
  child's responses, 86–97
  concerning behaviors and, 84
  concern verbalized in, 130
  curiosity in, 84
  description of, 75
  examples, 85–86, 131
  goal of, 83
  possibilities, 86
  voice given to child in, 84
episodes (challenging). *see also*
  waffle episode
  collaboration in problem-
    solving of, 74, 140, 185
  of great frequency, 58
  plans used to defuse, 146,
    194
  punishment and, 140
  Q&A, 145–146
  school issues and, 205
*Essential Conversation: What
  Parents and Teachers Can
  Learn from Each Other, The,*
  223
expectations
  concerning behaviors and, 72
  demanding rapid compliance
    with, 64

  disparities in, 173, 174
  Plan A and, 74
  Plan B and, 192
  problems adjusting, 33
  Q&A, 80
  at school, 207, 208
  setting aside, 77
  unrealistic (frustration with),
    187
expectations, difficulty
  meeting, 10, 12, 123. *see
  also* unsolved problems
  awareness of number of
    expectations, 47
  communication of, 14, 16
  concerning behaviors
    exhibited with, 37, 173
  Empathy step and, 115
  identification of expectations,
    15
  ignoring of behaviors
    accompanying, 63
  parental agreement on
    expectations, 194
  problems to be solved, 22
  relationship with child and,
    234
  situational factor of, 204

Faber, Adele, 183
family, 171–202
  challenges, 171
  communication patterns
    (family), 183–189
  communication problems,
    172
  concerning behaviors in, 171,
    172, 174
  example, 195–202

ABOUT THE AUTHOR

ROSS W. GREENE, PH.D., is a clinical psychologist and the originator of the innovative, evidence-based approach called *Collaborative & Proactive Solutions* (CPS), as described in this book. He also developed and executive produced the award-winning documentary film *The Kids We Lose*, released in 2018. Dr. Greene was on the faculty at Harvard Medical School for more than twenty years and founded the nonprofit Lives in the Balance in 2009. He is currently adjunct professor in the Department of Psychology at Virginia Tech and adjunct professor in the Faculty of Science at the University of Technology in Sydney, Australia. Dr. Greene has worked with several thousand behaviorally challenging kids and their caregivers, and he and his colleagues have overseen implementation and evaluation of the CPS model in hundreds of schools, inpatient psychiatry units, and residential and juvenile detention facilities, with dramatic effect: significant reductions in recidivism, discipline referrals, detentions, suspensions, and use of restraint and seclusion. Dr. Greene lectures throughout the world and lives in Freeport, Maine.